Doctor Watson Architecture

PROPOSITIONS
The Architecture School

A prototypical design for a new kind of architecture school

Victoria Watson

An AIR Grid Publication
Copyright © 2024, Doctor VA Watson

ISBN: 9781838018047

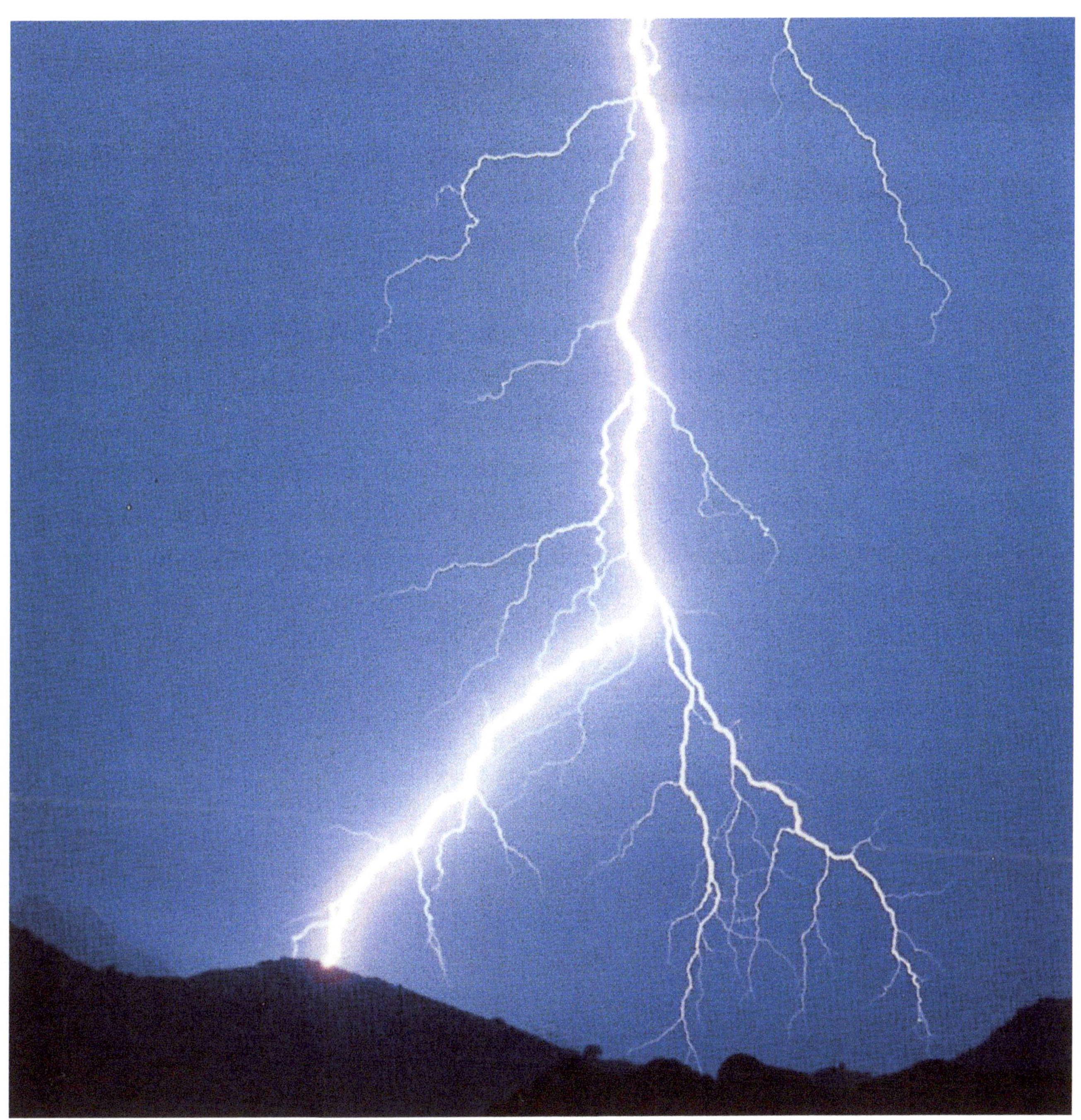

Jove terrified a few giants into becoming humans with his thunderbolts

Preamble

The idea for a new kind of architecture school began when, at the turn of the millennium, we were invited by David Greene and Samantha Hardingham to contribute to the prospectus for their speculative idea for an Invisible University. Our response to the call was a tiny bit nonsensical but we are reproducing it here in unedited form, as a kind of barometer of the mood of the times.

Air Studio, Invisible University: Contribution to a Prospectus

Location

•In the name of 'freedom' the official instrument of education (the University) offers its students 'choice'. •In the language of the University the vehicle of student choice is termed the 'free elective module' (FEM); ironically the FEM is allowed to form but a single component of the students education, thus giving rise to a number of interesting questions concerning the status of the remaining components; are these to be understood as 'compulsorily non-elected modules' (CnEM), i.e., as the obligatory imperatives of officially recognised education? •Floating on the back of a number of FEM's, the Air Studio, although invisible, is advantageously located within the educational infrastructure of a specific London university. Perhaps cruelly, the true identity of the Air Studio is kept secret from all enlisted students, only those able to feel the aerial forces will instinctively realize it is not 'freedom' they are investigating on their freely chosen FEM but the underlying electromagical constituents of being: Charm.

Thesis

1. The Air Studio operates within the brittle folds of a psychic disturbance embedded within the 'normality' of architectural education. With the demise of the 'grand narrative' what is there to teach; is architecture reduced to mere illustration? In such shoddy circumstances is it the task of the architect to transform delineation into representation, achievable through the efficient rendering of surfaces?

2. In a short text written in the early years of the twentieth century, the architect of Suprematism, Kazimir Malevich stated:

The relation of Suprematism to materials is contrary to the presently growing propaganda for a culture of materials, the call for esthetics. The treatment of the surfaces of the material appears to be a psychosis of contemporary artists.

For all the rich complexity of computer space, the contemporary student of architecture is enthrall to the render zone. We have chosen to work with air because, being a material without surfaces, it resists the lure of the rendering package. Air is very thin matter, the higher up into the atmosphere you go, the thinner it gets.

3. Yves Klein's project for the Architecture of the Air aimed to put living bodies inside the space of representation. By substituting a tangible invisible - air - for the mathematical invisible of perspective construction, Klein's investigations pointed the way toward a total theatricalisation of nature, the world revealed as one, huge, environmental painting. But the weakest point in Klein's argument is precisely within that register of production most consistently linked with architecture, namely building. Lacking knowledge and self-assurance in this area of production, Klein's instinctual ability - which in general he could depend upon to connect to the primal sounds of preverbal speech - appears to have abandoned him whenever he came face to face with the matter of building. Thus, we would argue; Klein did not take the Architecture of the Air as far as it could go, he left his project incomplete and therefore open for further thought, research experimentation and speculation.

4. In the 'prismatic towers' and 'free-span pavilions' of the concluding years of his productive life, Mies van der Rohe took his dream of an architecture of 'skin and bones' to its logical, alarming and at the same time extraordinarily electromagical conclusion. Mies' skin & bone structures stand as a testament to the inherent duality of 'constructive thought': not the differentiation of an opposition between mind and matter but the vital electromagical forces binding skin and bone into a unitary form. But in order to create unitary form, Mies had to concentrate so hard on the spatial aspect of construction that he almost totally annihilated time; which is why his buildings are so silent and so still. And it is why they serve, so effectively, as surfaces, tracing the changes of the air around them, the clouds and the wind and the passing of day into night. Ephemeral and lovely though these qualities are, they are nevertheless a distraction, undermining the sensible evocation of a 'clearing at the limit of chaos'.

Syllabus
•The temporal fabric of human environments is bounded by measurement and matter, but measurement and matter are not of themselves inherently binding; it is a question of attitudes, particularly of those embedded in decision making institutions and processes.
•Students of the Air Studio will remain unaware of the parallel existence of the Invisible University and of the fact they are studying architecture through air and not the other way round - the unacknowledged norm. To the students, the syllabus they follow will seem to have been set down by the host institution. However unbeknownst, the syllabus of the Air Studio is, in truth, as follows:

•The Air Studio adopts a cautious and inquisitive approach to the study of measure and matter.

•Working with air – the vital matter in which human & nonhuman measurements are made – students of the Air Studio will follow a course of structured project work. The range of investigative strategies totals nine, each one aimed to investigate air through a different aspect of its complex materiality (see list of aerial orientations below).

•It is of no consequence if students work as individuals or in groups; however, it is essential to the success of the Studio that the project work be pursued in a spirit of research, that is through structured, goal-orientated inquiry, with a conscious sensibility toward electromagical objectivity and cosmic poetry.

•List of Aerial Orientations:

1. Flight
2. Wings
3. Wind
4. Falling
5. Ascending
6. Blue sky
7. Constellations
8. Nebula
9. Silence

•Each orientation is worth one credit: Level 01 – three air credits: Bachelor of the Air; Level 02 – six air credits: Master of the Air; Level 03 – nine air credits: Flying Doctor

•Just as students remain unaware of their invisible affiliations, so they will remain unaware of their ascent status (level). Hints may be communicated by means of small prizes and gifts, pencils, rubber stamps with encrypted congratulations and the publication of certain exemplary pieces of work in the Air Studio's dedicated magazine: Flying Circus.

Recommendation

Occasionally, one smart student will guess. When this happens the student will be sent before the executive committee of the Invisible University with the highest recommendation they be admitted to the fraternity and with the full expectation they contribute a course of their own.

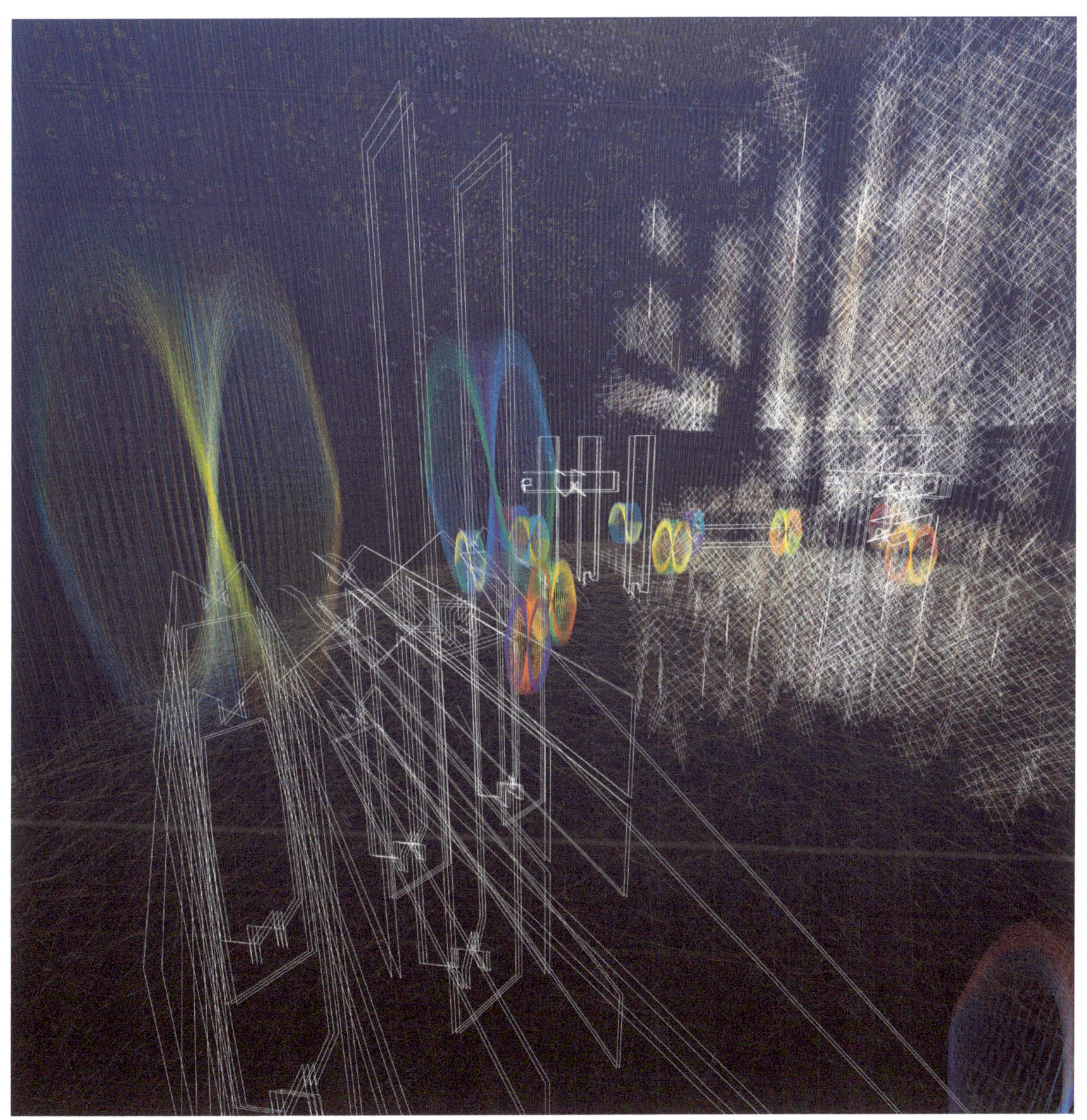

Posting from the Vitruvian forest

Introduction

The School of Architecture is a big, open building defined by a lightweight, transparent and permeable enclosing device - the shell. The nature of the shell, its configuration and material manifestation, is such that it will foster a close coupling between the school and the greater world outside.

By encouraging the variety and the variability of the outer world to permeate the school the aim is to encourage an attitude of active participation between architectural education and the contemporary cultural condition. One way in which it is proposed to do this is by incorporating a public train station inside the architecture school, another way is by using the rail facility to take the work of the school out on tour.

A wide underpass dives under the tracks, forging a link between the two sides. On one side of the track is a miniature Italian piazza where a number of the school's services are housed in a group of discrete buildings arranged around an urban forum. These buildings are available for teaching and learning about architecture as a multiplicity of public occasions, rather than for the exclusive use of the internal school community. Besides the station and piazza there is a long, open-frame structure with platforms on top and this serves as the workshop and studio space, where the students make work. A gantry system links the studio structure to the rail-system and special carriages can be assembled and fed into the rail network as rolling exhibitions of architectural ideas.

Detail thinking about the school curriculum and nature of teaching environments are left out of consideration at this early, design stage, which is concentrated instead on the physical structures of the school. We did this because we believe curriculum and teaching environment should be subject to a constantly evolving discourse and as such remain too fluid to be embodied in fixed forms.

We call the components of such discourses Postings from the Vitruvian Forest, here is one of our favourites:

During the 18th century, when the idea of architecture in the disciplinary sense that we know it today began to stabilise, a great deal of intellectual effort went into thinking about origins. In order to grasp the novelty of 18th century work on origins we have to begin by looking at the idea of origins that had been inherited from antiquity and had remained, more or less, intact up until the 18th century. The oldest remaining treatise on architecture was written in the first century BCE by the Roman architect Vitruvius and it was dedicated to the emperor Augustus, it is called The Ten Books of Architecture. In Book I Vitruvius states, the fundamental

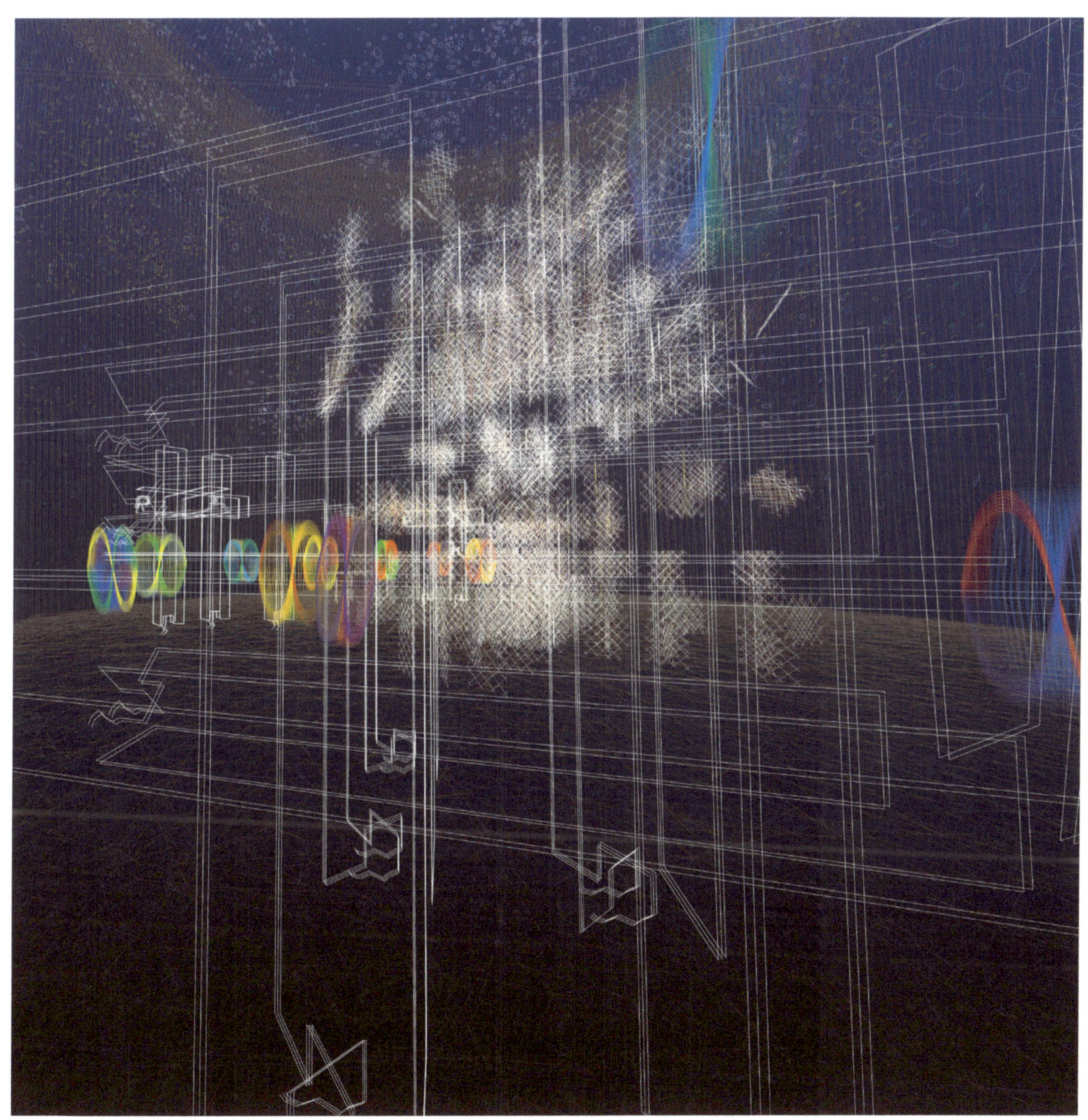

The habit of building arose amongst the first humans purely by chance

principles of architecture, are Order, Arrangement, Eurhythmy, Symmetry, Propriety and Economy, it is significant that Vitruvius begins his treatise by stating the principles of architecture, but he does not regard these as equivalent to architecture's origins, to find out about the origins the reader has to wait until they get to Book II.

In book II Vitruvius explains how the principles of architecture were discovered, thanks to the development of a habit of building amongst primeval human groups. Prior to their acquisition of the habit of building, Vitruvius' humans were little more than animals, a curious species whose individual members lived on their own. The habit of building arose amongst the first humans purely by chance: a thunderbolt, cast down from the sky, caused a sudden outbreak of fire in the forest where the humans lived. Terrified by the ferocity of the fire, the humans ran away. But as the fire subsided the humans came back into the forest and, timidly approaching the subsiding flames, found how pleasurable it was to gather together around the warm, glowing embers. As they were gathered around the fire so the humans began to make signs to one another, indicating their pleasure and enjoyment. Charmed by the quieted fire, the humans learned how to tend it and to keep it alive. According to Vitruvius then, it was thanks to the accident of the forest fire that the humans began to take pleasure in one another's company and so to form a community.

Once assembled in this way, the humans found they could agree upon articulate sounds and they began to indicate by name things in common use, which is how they began to talk and eventually to converse with one another. Speech is perhaps the most notable system of representation distinguishing human societies from the societies of other animals, ants for example. As well as being able to speak, the humans began to realise they differed from the other animals in other ways too, they realised that they could walk upright and so were able to raise their eyes and gaze up at the stars. Gazing into the stars is another form of behaviour that human creatures engage in and that clearly distinguishes them from other animals. The sky at night is a wonderful place for learning to recognise patterns and to begin to exercise the facility for abstract thinking. The humans also realised that walking upright meant they could work easily with their hands and fingers and, according to Vitruvius, coincident with their beginning to read the night sky, the humans began to construct shelters and so began the art of mediating abstract thoughts through material forms. Through his tale of origins Vitruvius suggests, unlike other animals, the human desire to build is something the creatures acquire only after they have begun to live in a society. But actually, even if he does not press the point, Vitruvius is saying more than that, he is suggesting the foundation of human society is coincident with the emergence of two forms of communication, these being speech and building.

Vitruvius lists a number of what we would today call material practices that arise as a consequence of the activity

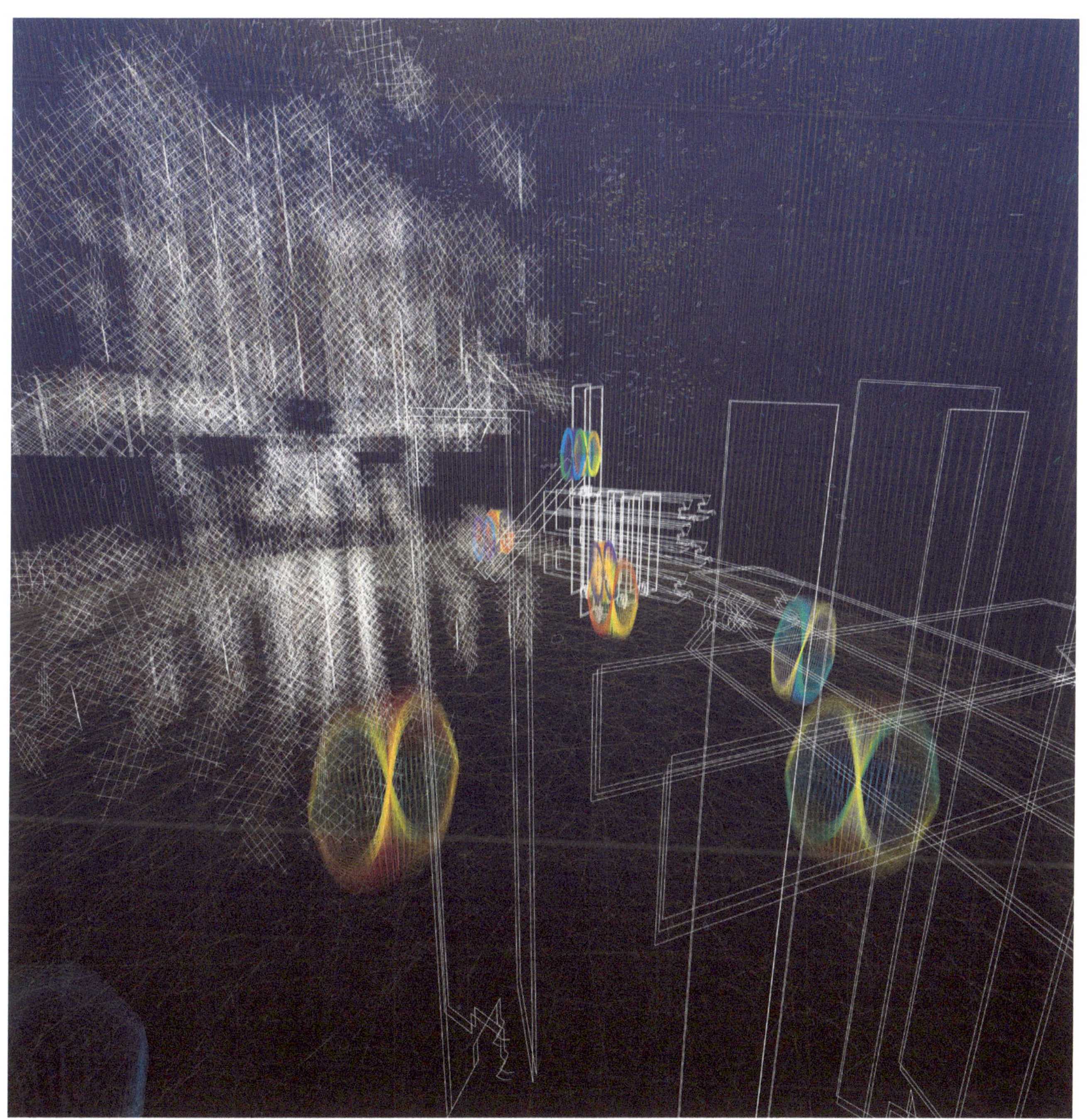

Vitruvius' humans had not yet discovered architecture

of building, he describes these acts of building in some detail:

Some made them of green boughs, others dug caves on mountainsides, and some, in imitation of the nests of swallows and the way they built, made places of refuge out of mud and twigs. Next, by observing the shelters of others and adding new details to their own inceptions, they constructed better and better kinds of huts as time went on.

Because the humans could speak to one another so they were able to develop a language for talking about building, thereby developing knowledge of building, and to form ideas about building in their minds, which they could test in new acts of building - the production and use of knowledge to change the way we do things is today called improvement, or progress. But even with the ability to reflect upon their work, Vitruvius' humans had not yet discovered architecture; there were still two more stages to go. First, knowledge of building had to advance to the point where the humans were able to predetermine the forms they were building with greater and greater precision; with this advance they stopped building huts and began to build houses, with foundations and brick or stonewalls and roofs made of timber and tiles. Vitruvius believed the passage from huts into houses corresponded to the entry into a new mode of life, a life that was civilised and it was not until they entered into civilisation that the humans were able to recognise the fundamental principles of architecture: *Order, Arrangement, Eurhythmy, Symmetry, Propriety and Economy.*

Although Vitruvius does not say so, it is implicit in his theory that the principles of architecture, once discovered, need not be restricted to the formation of huts, houses and civic structures, such as temples and basilicas but can be utilised across a wide range of practices. Hence Vitruvius includes the making of timepieces and the construction of machinery as works of architecture. Following Vitruvius then, it is simply incorrect to associate the principles of architecture with building alone, architecture might have evolved out of the art of building, but once discovered it provides a set of autonomous mental facilities, which are available for all sorts of creative activities.

But perhaps even more important than that, we discover from Vitruvius' story how architecture's preoccupation with origins digs deeper than the building of huts but is rooted in the coincidence of language and building; which are in turn born of the unified pleasures of feeling comfortable and communicating and sharing that feeling with others. Or to put it another way, architecture originates neither from comfort nor community but from the entanglement of both.

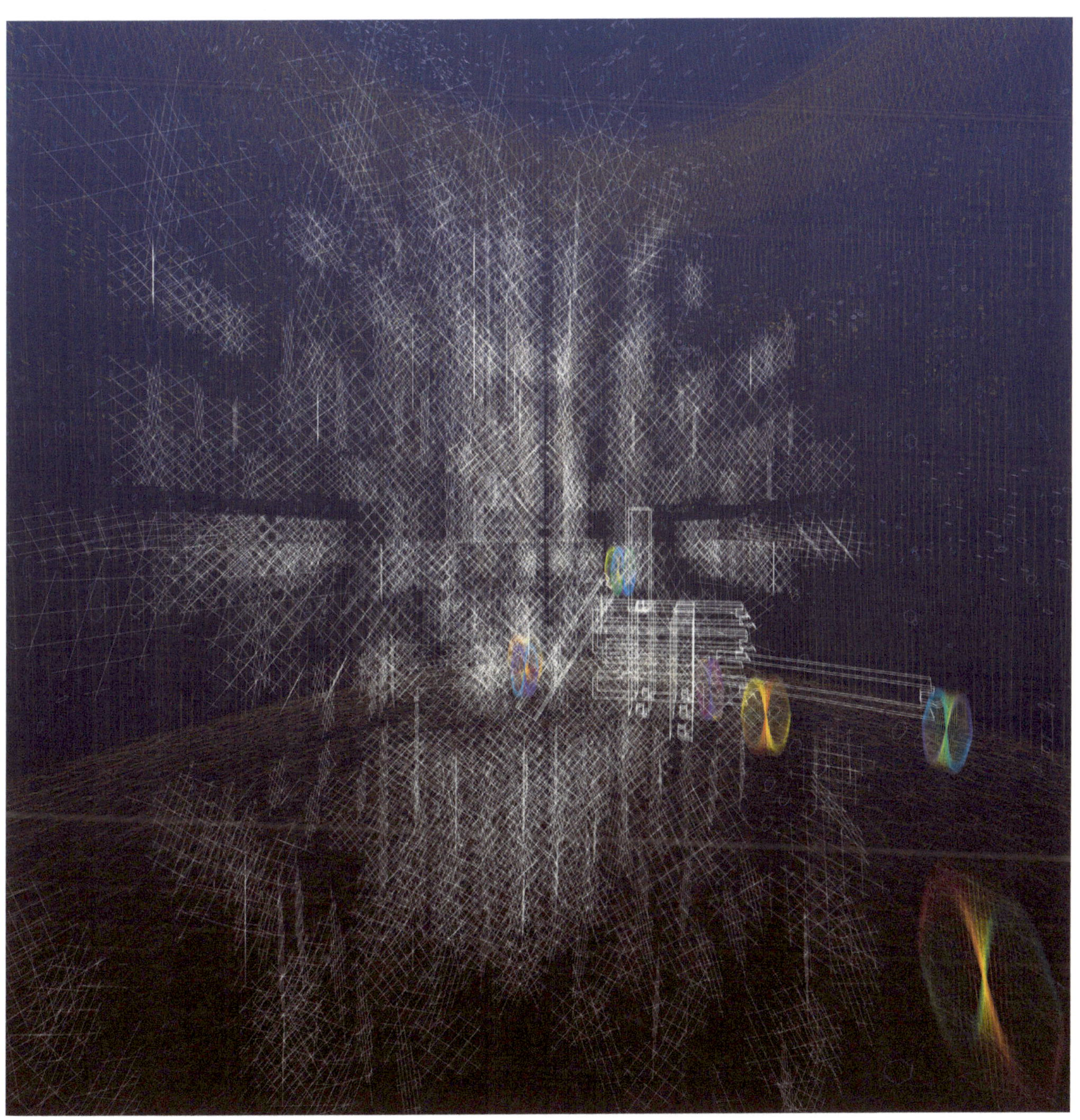

Neither comfort nor communication but the entanglement of both

Comparison of Relative Sizes

top left, diameter of the dome of the Pantheon, 2nd century Rome
top middle, plan footprint of the Crown Hall at IIT, Mies van der Rohe, 1950-'56
top right, plan footprint of Locomotivo, Aldo Rossi, 1962, (320 x 320 metres)
middle left, plan footprint of Chicago Convention Hall, Mies van der Rohe, 1953-'54
bottom right, plan footprint of the New Architecture School, (288 x 144 metres)

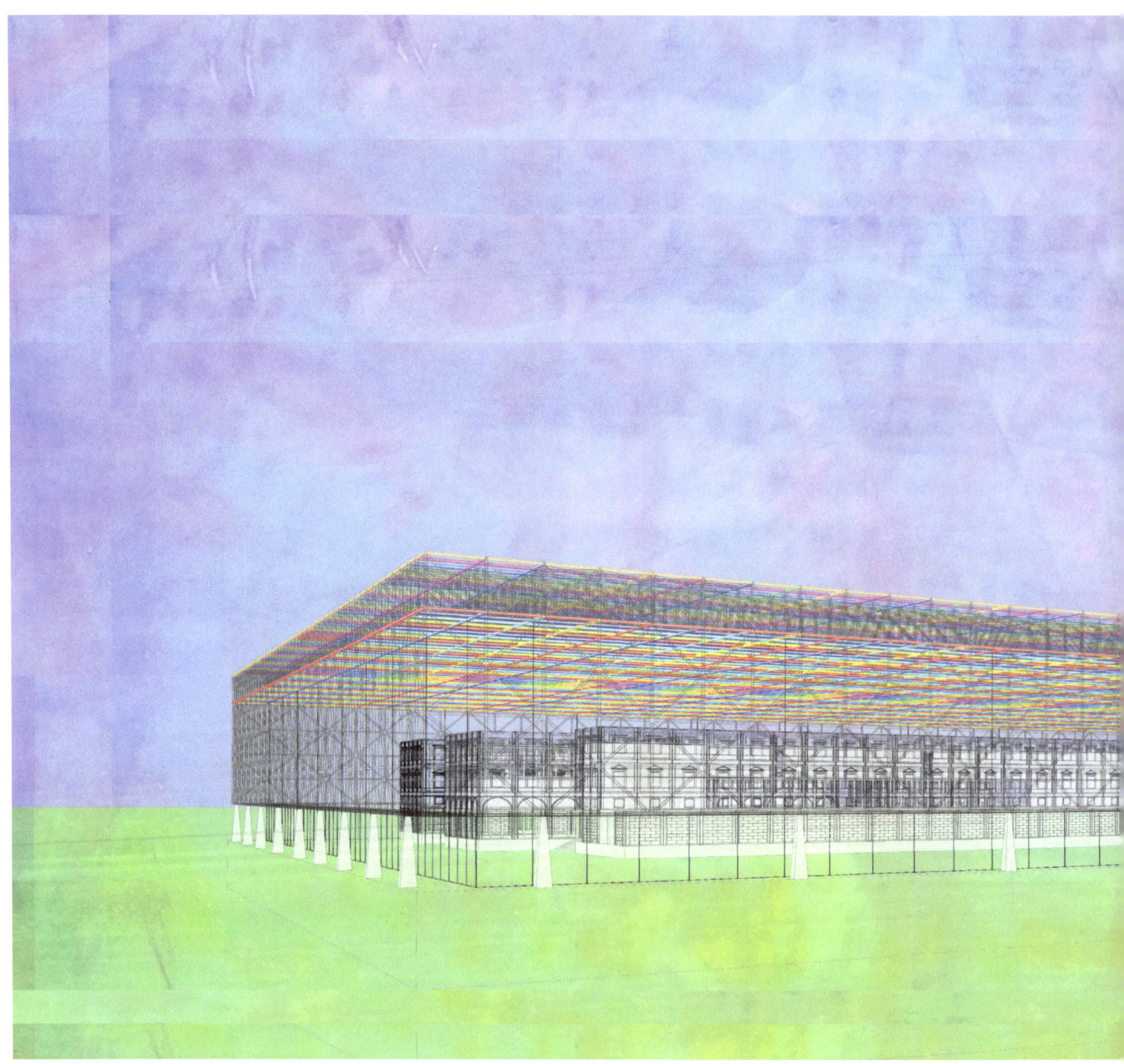

Figure 1. View of the new architecture school in a fictive setting

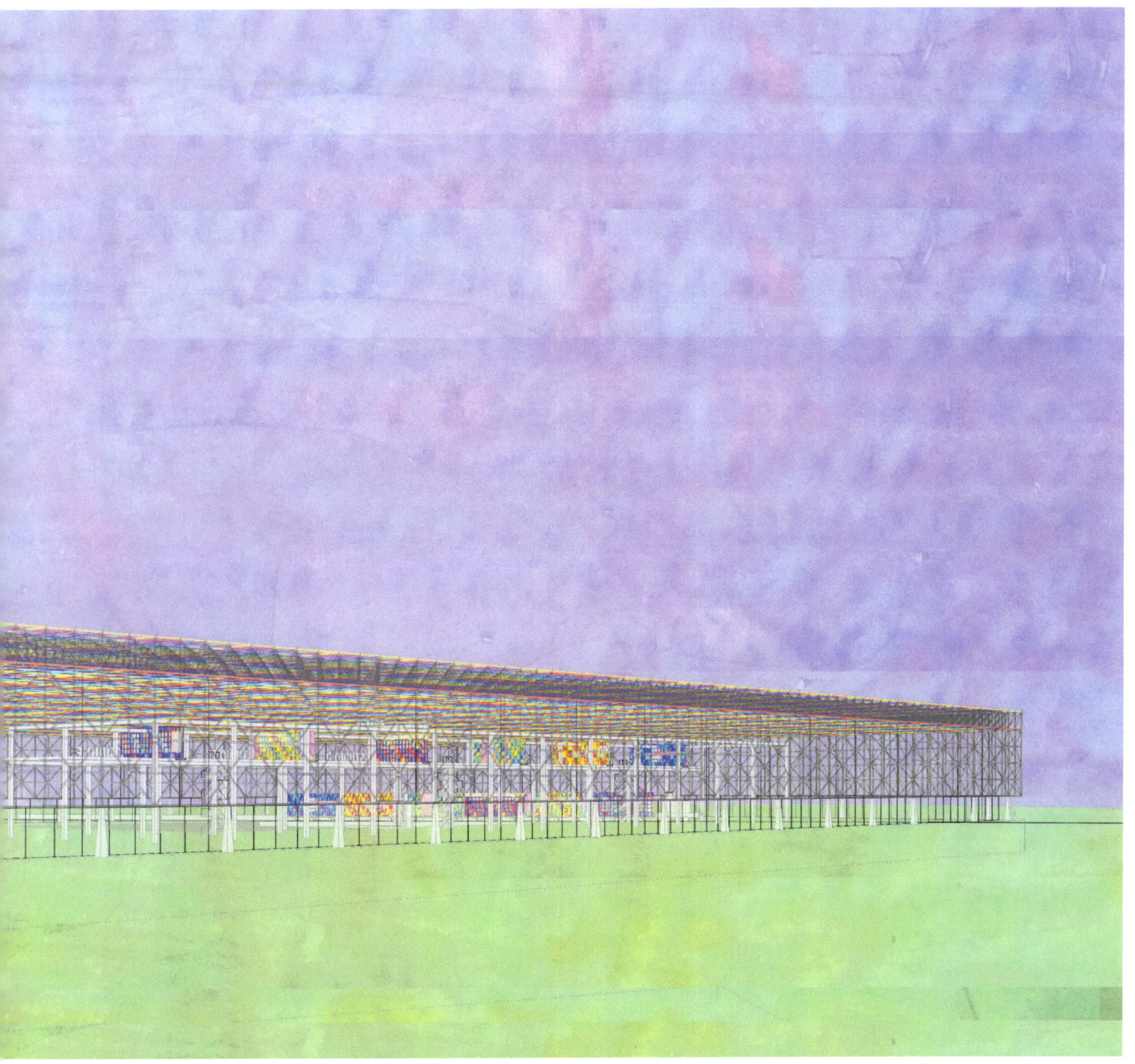

Figure 2. Basement plan & section aa (drawn at 1/500)

Figure 3. Ground floor plan & section bb (drawn at 1/500)

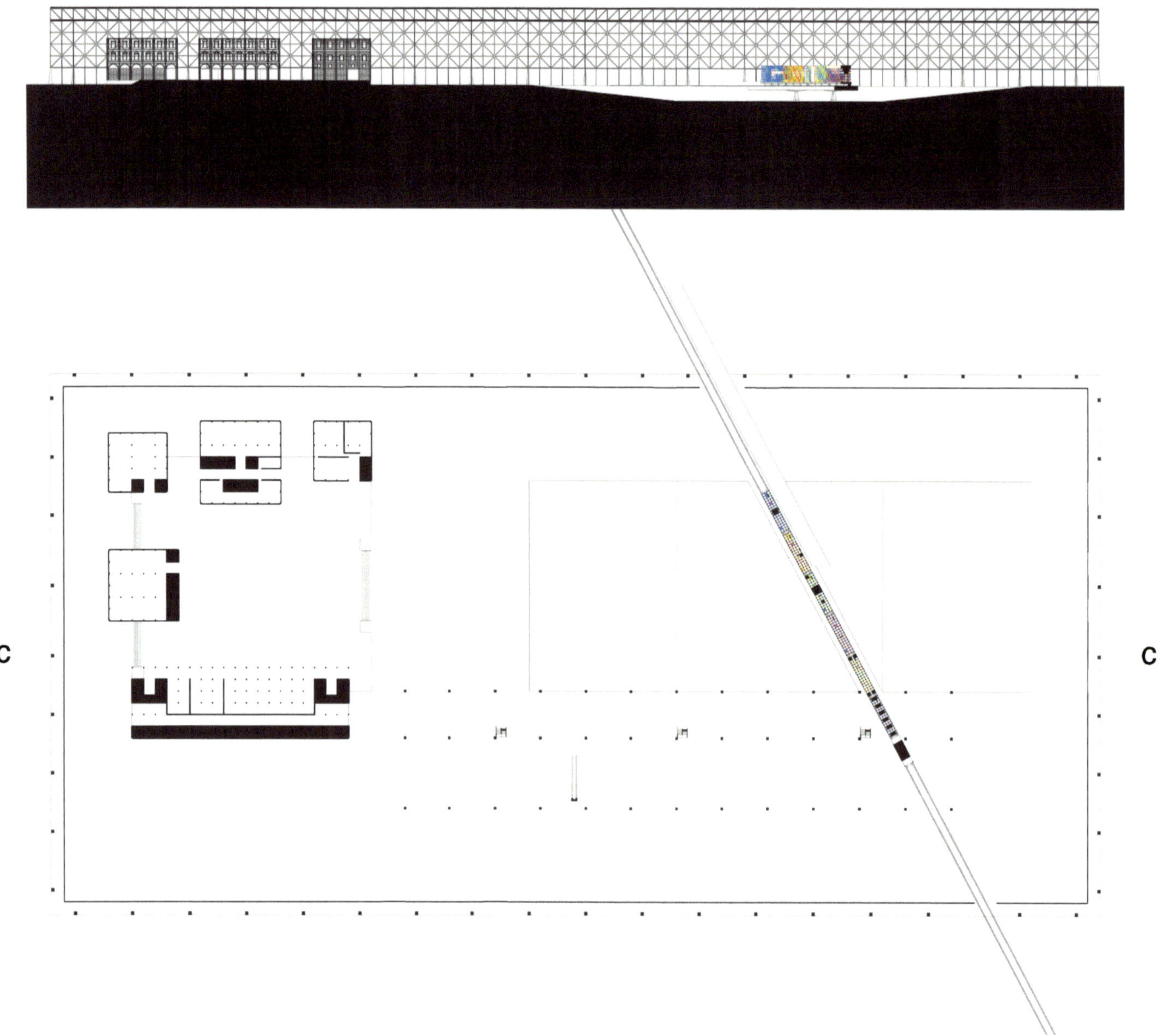

Figure 4. Piazza plan & section cc (drawn at 1/500)

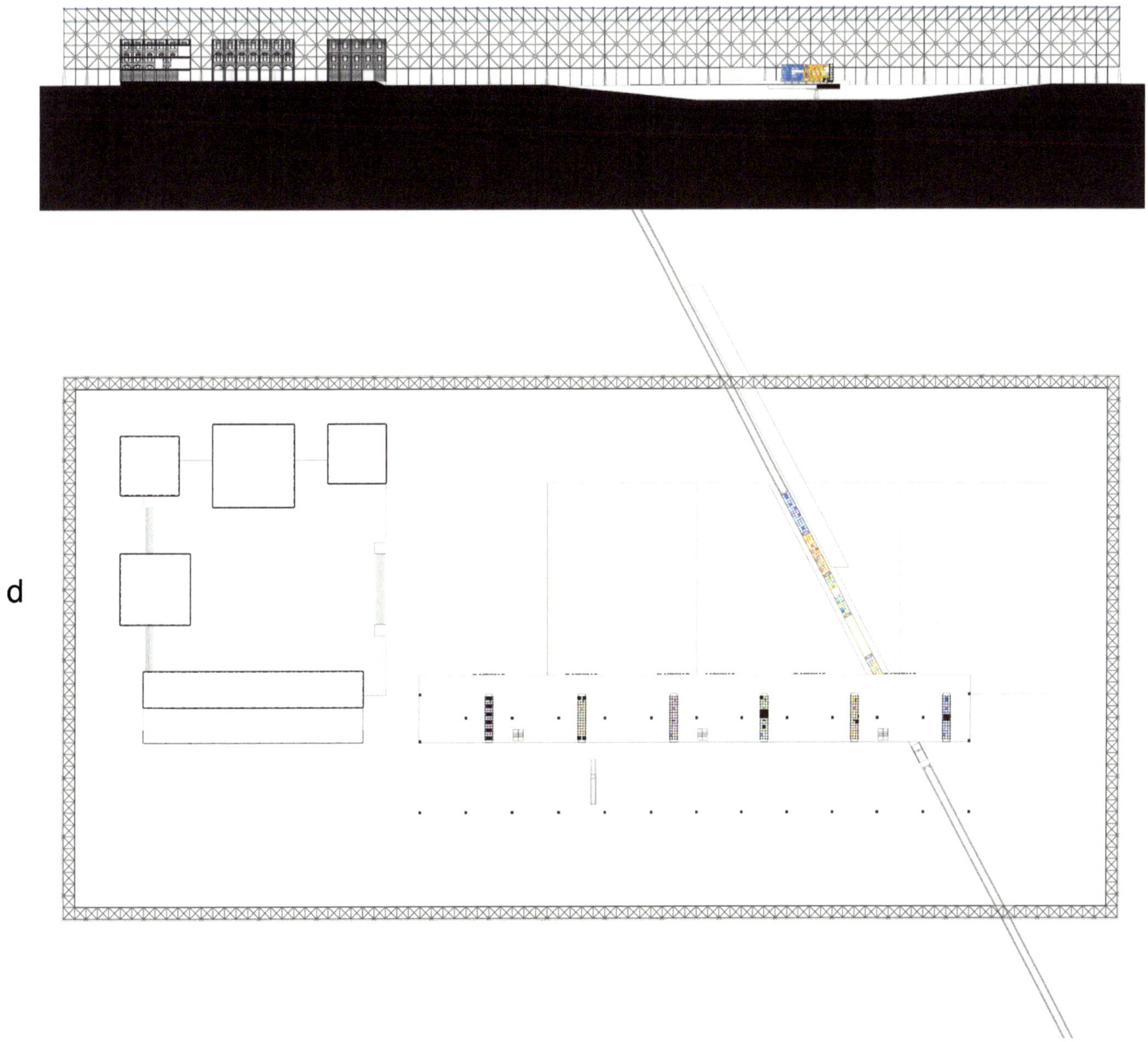

d

d

Figure 5. Loft plan & section dd (drawn at 1/500)

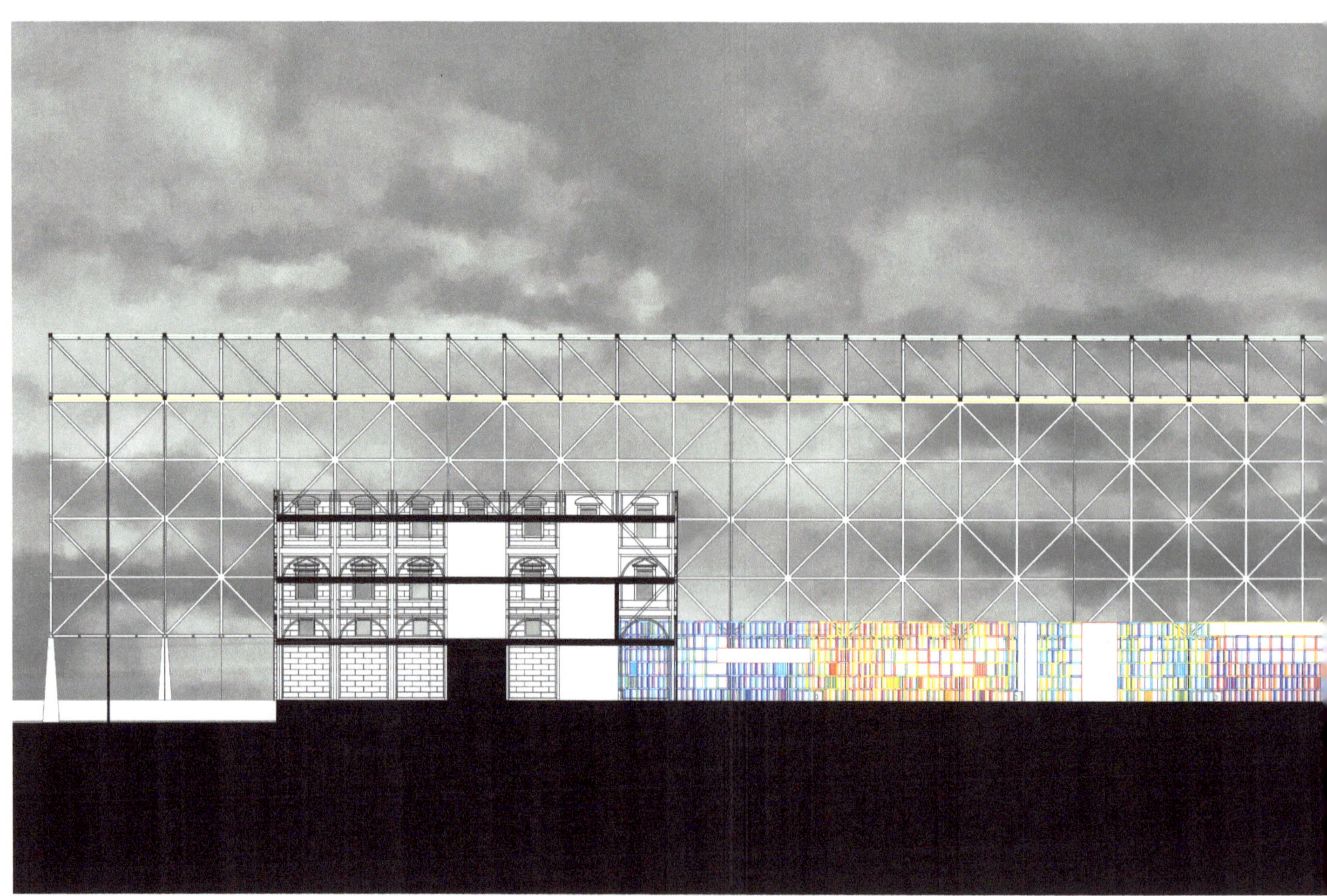

Figure 6. Short section through the piazza with service buildings either side (original drawn at 1/200)

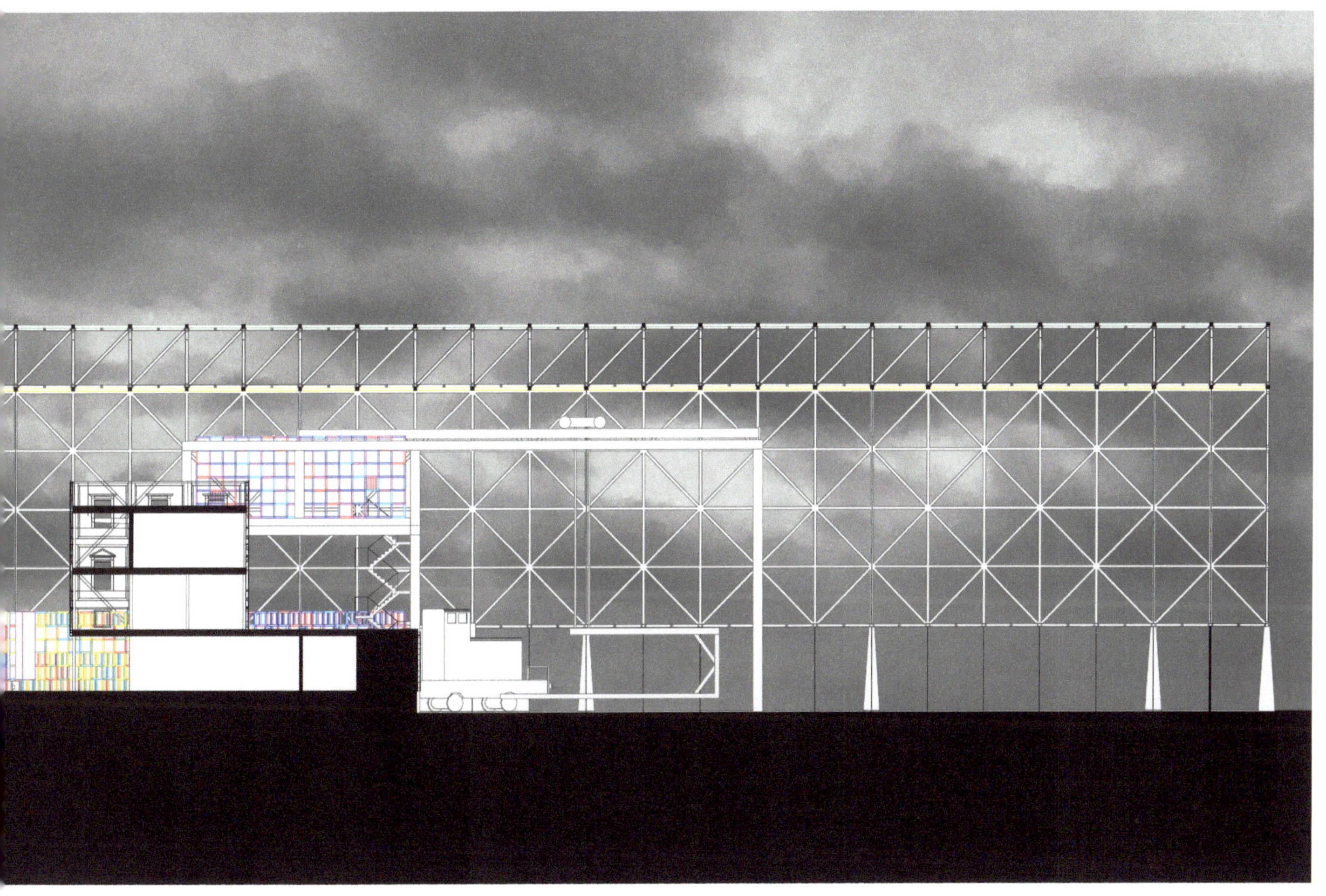

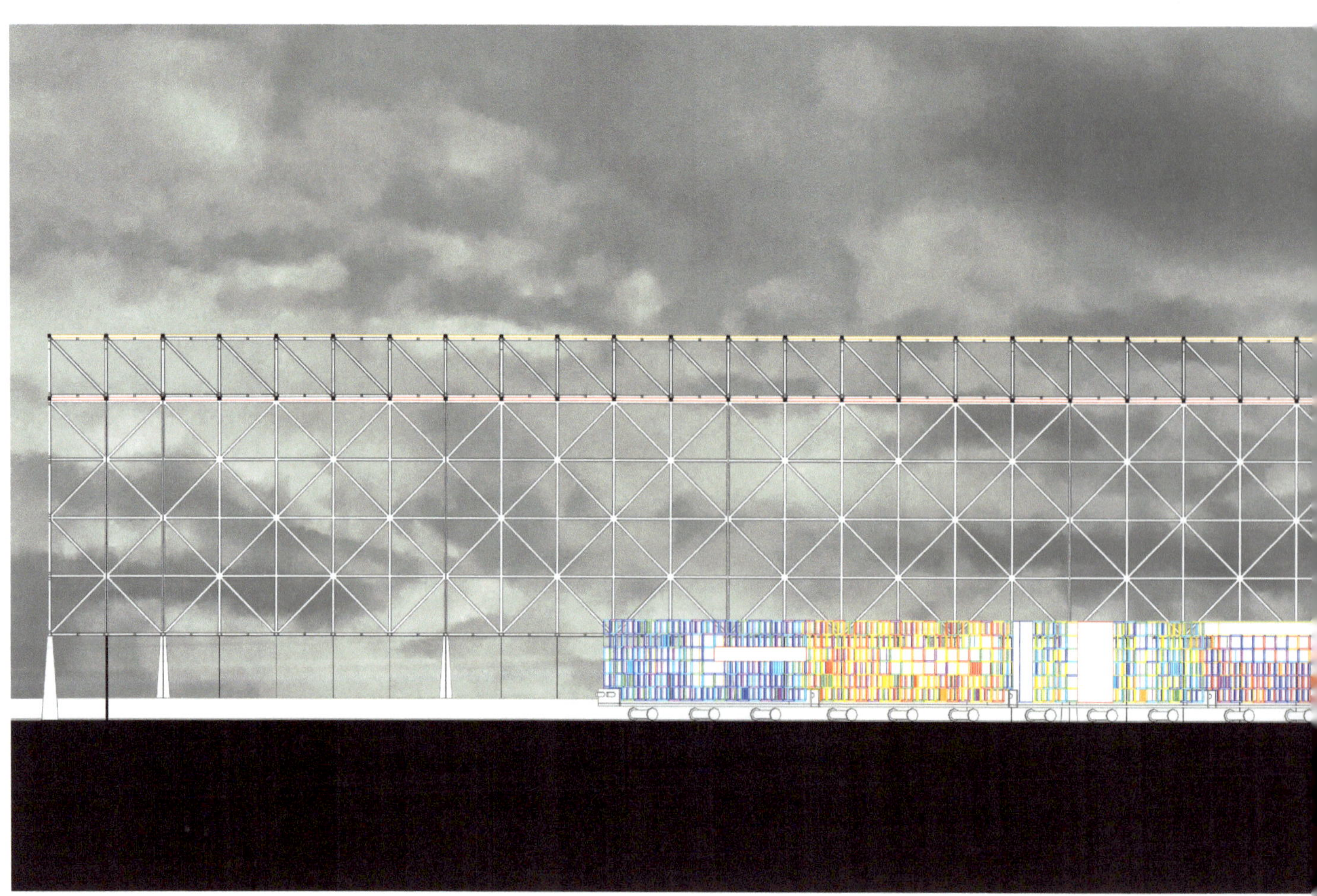

Figure 7. Short section through the studio and workshop structure (original drawn at 1/200)

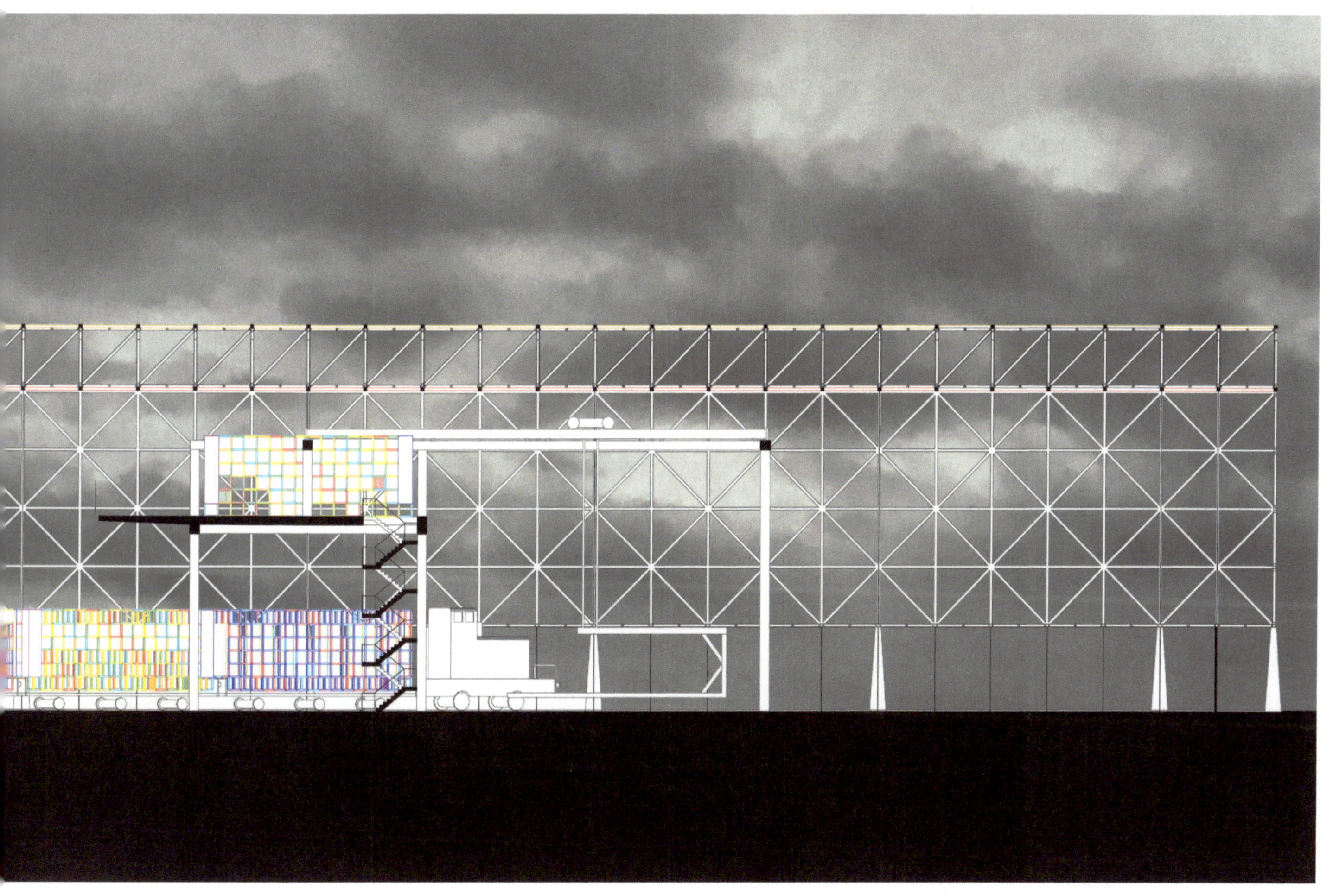

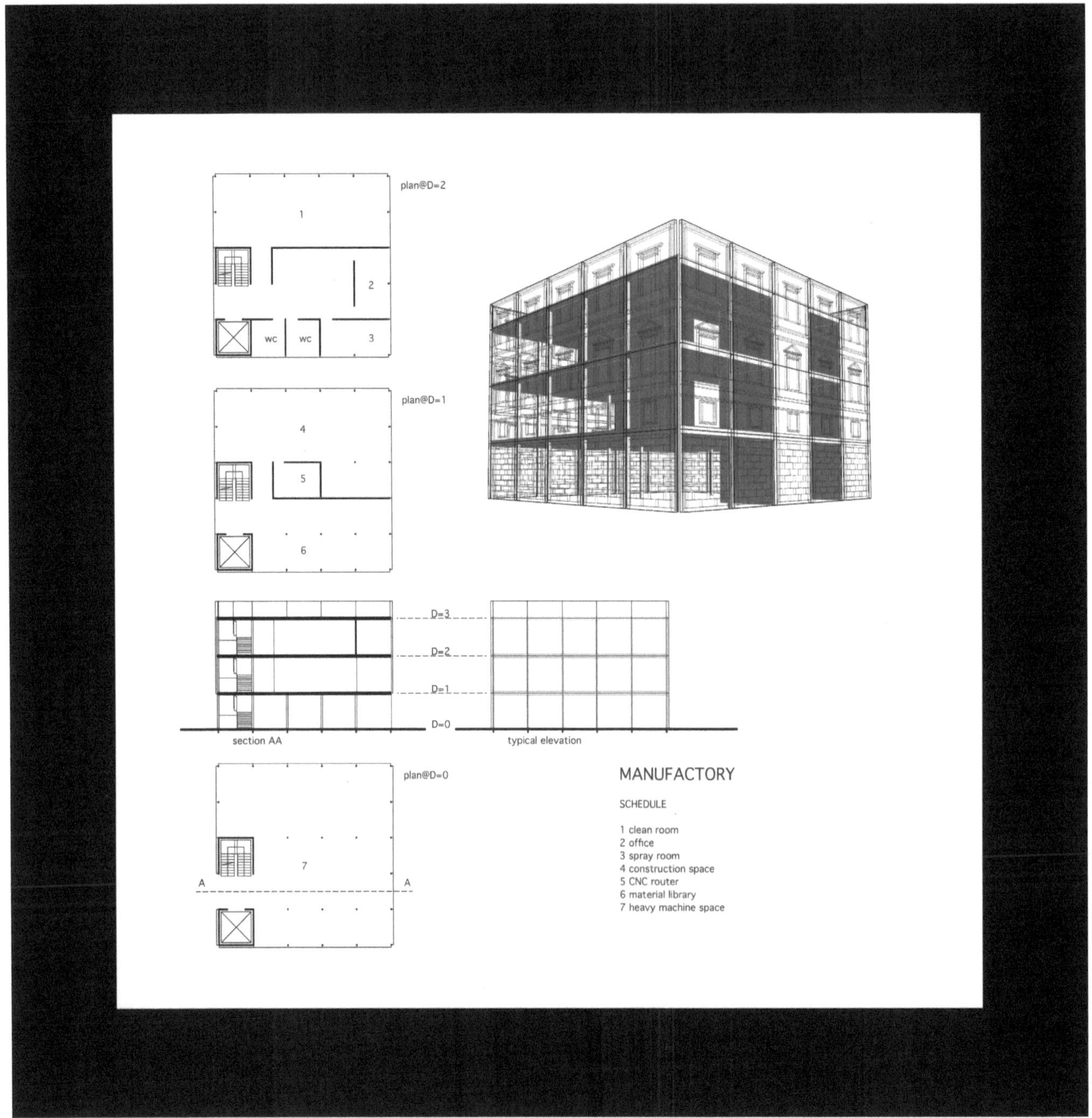

Figure 8. Service building: i) manufactory

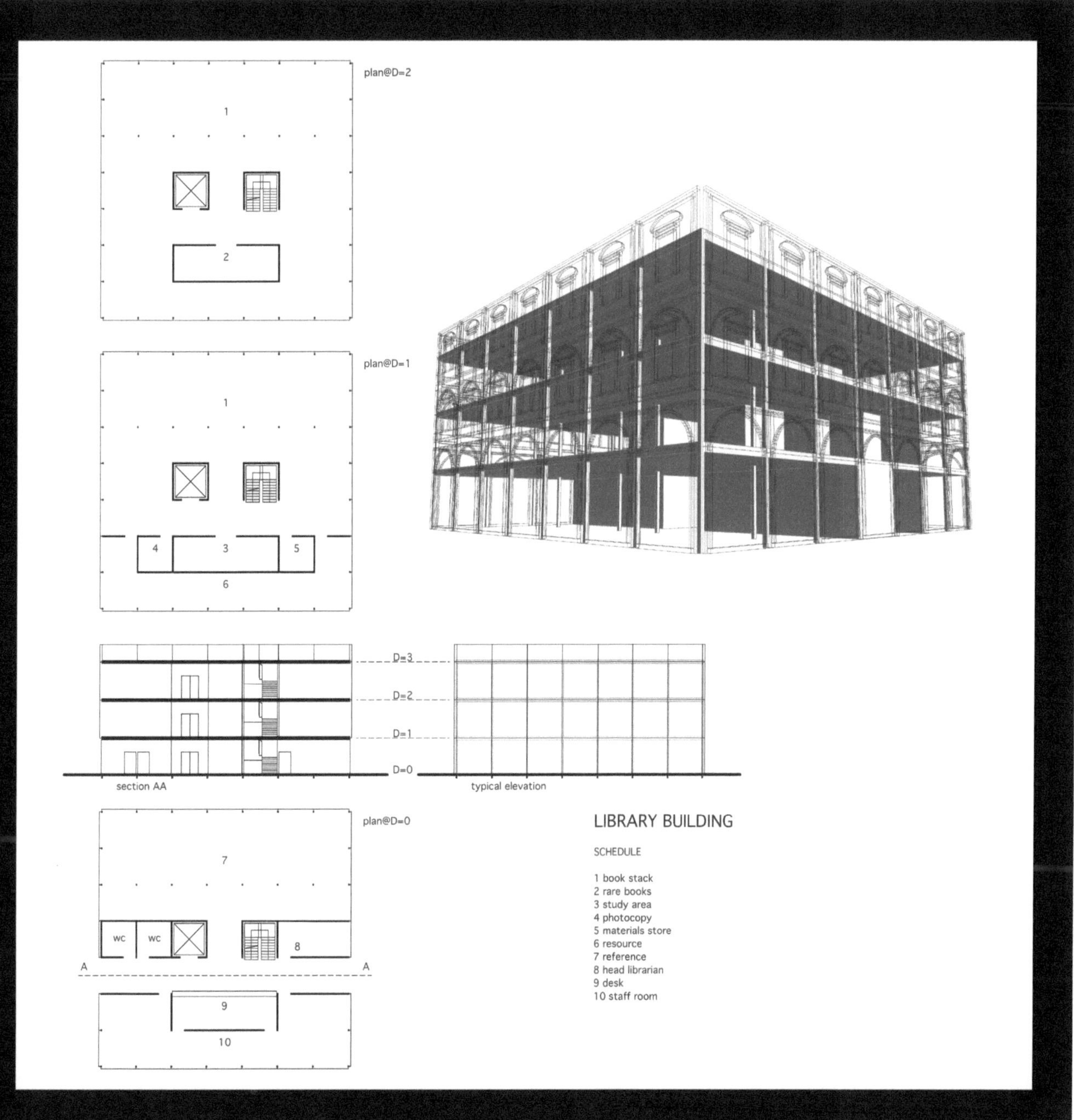

Figure 9. Service building: ii) library

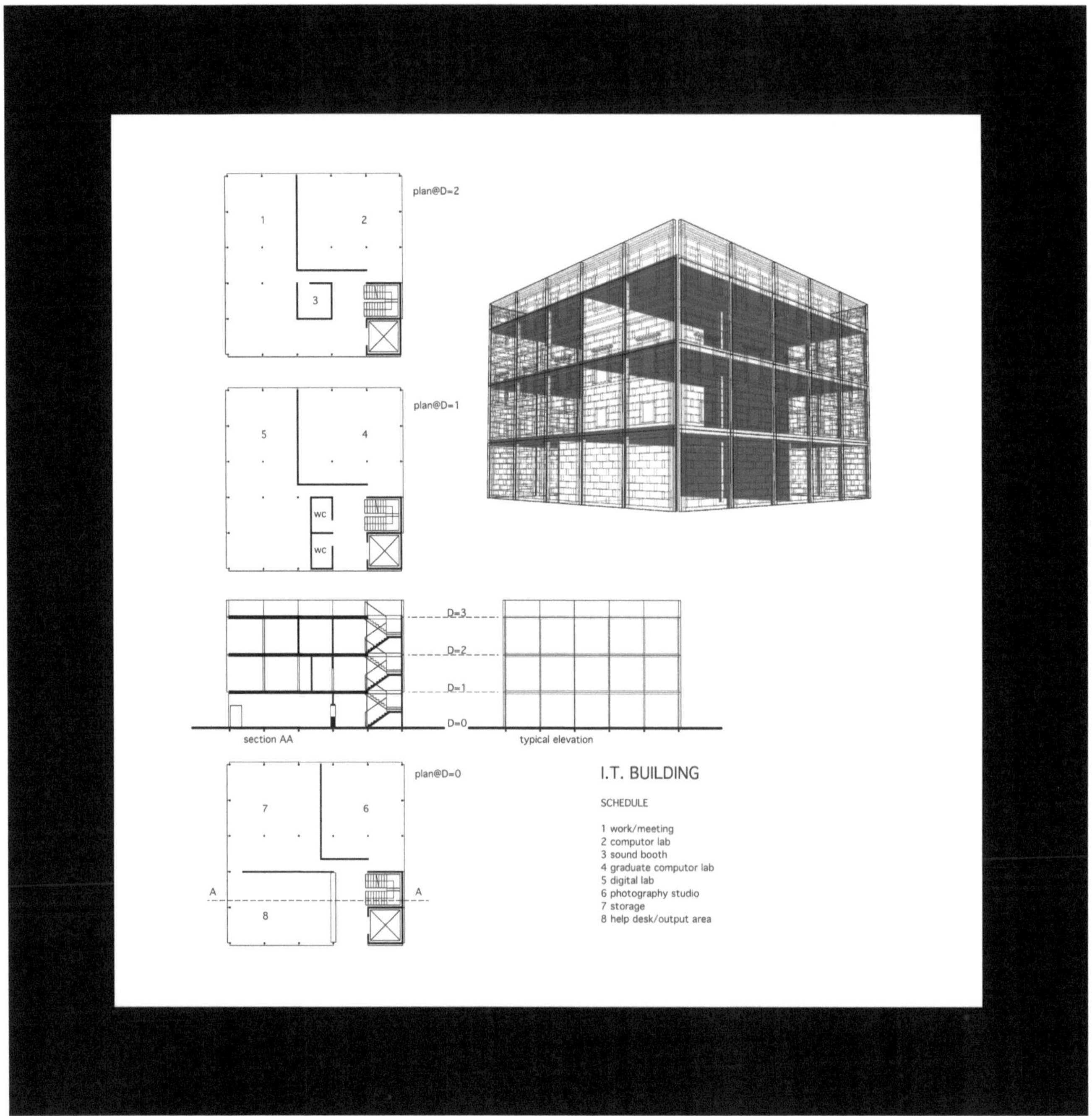

Figure 10. Service building: iii) IT building

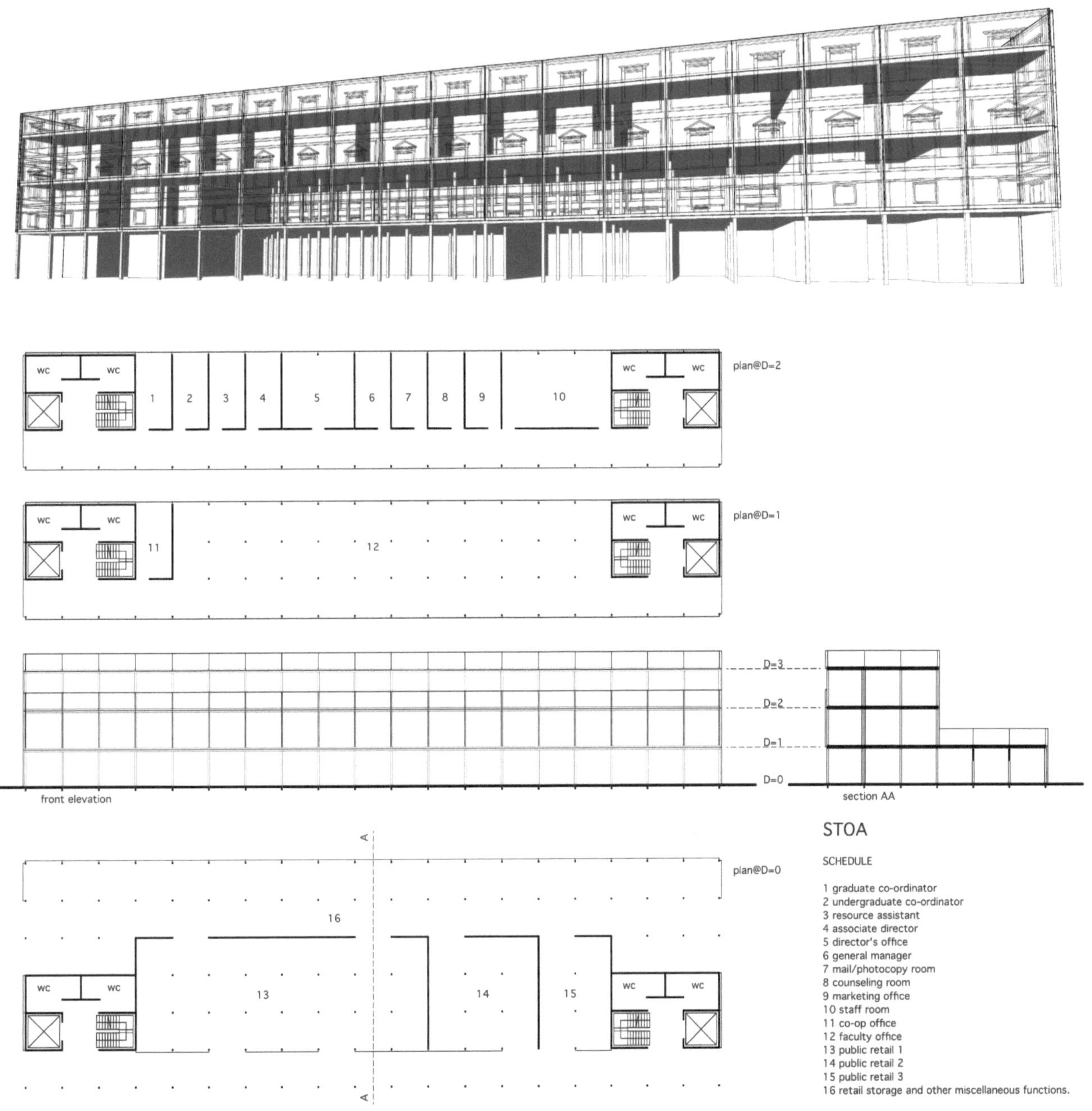

Figure 11. Service building: iv) stoa

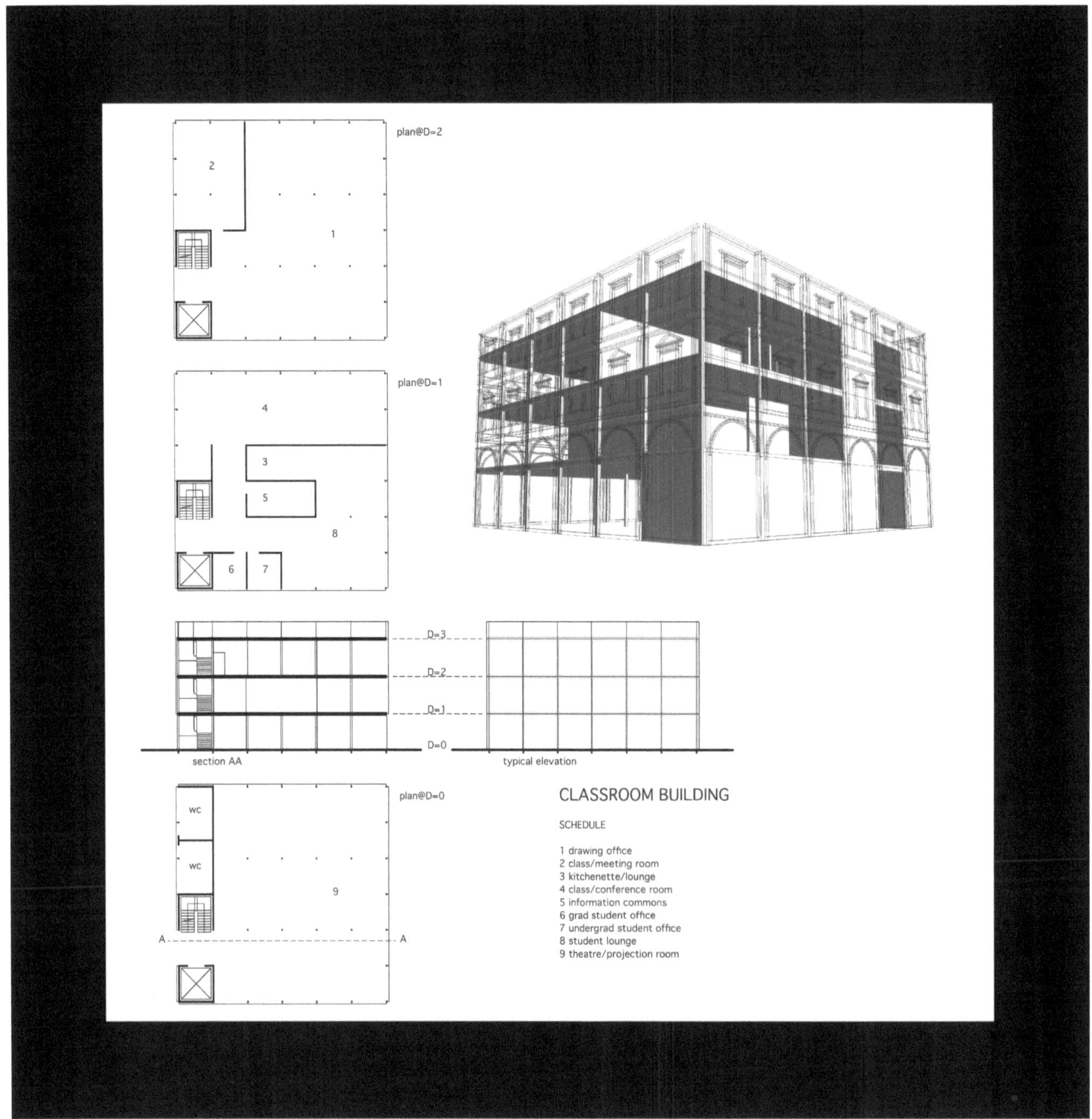

Figure 12. Service building: v) classroom block

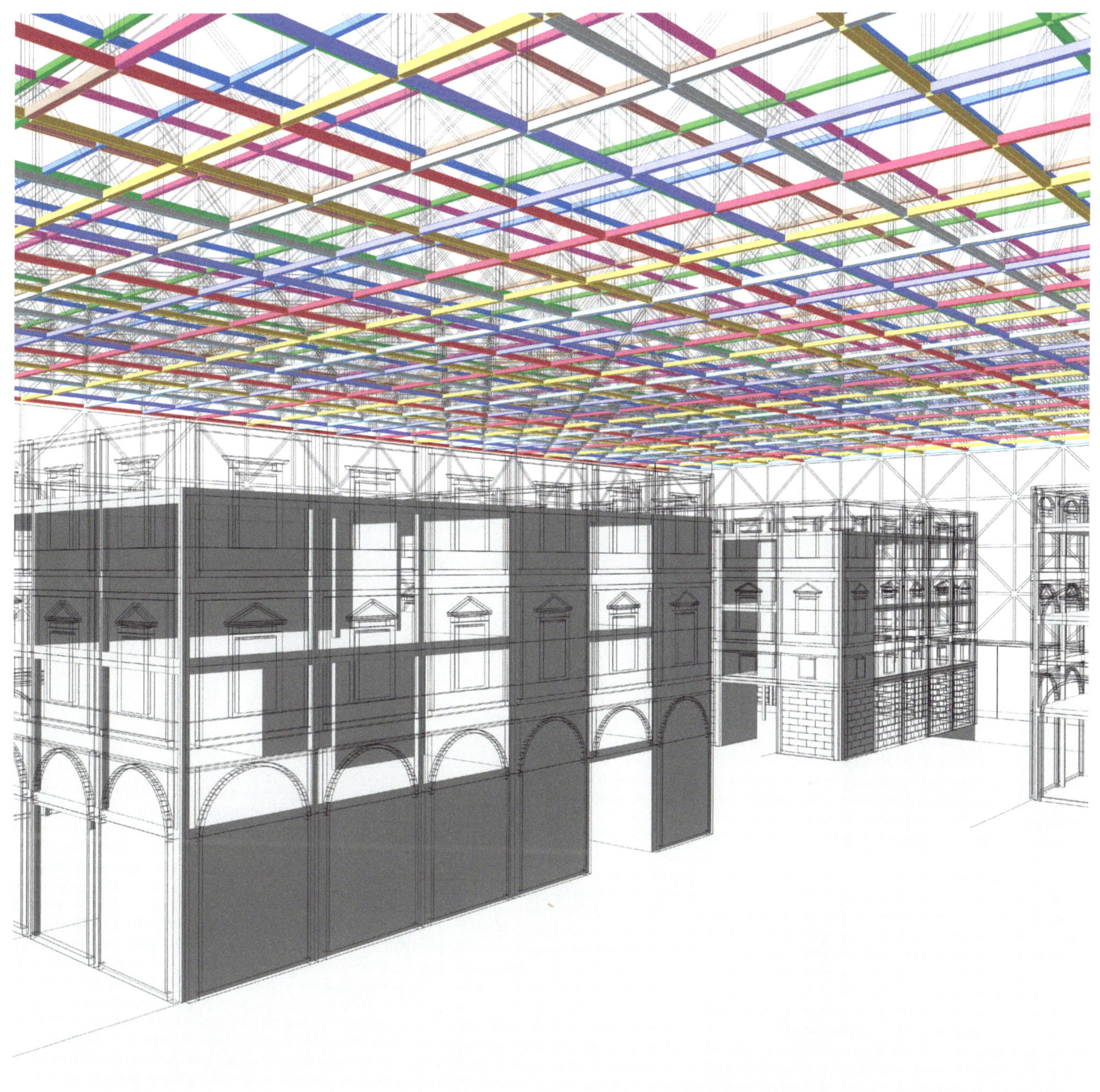

Figure 13. Looking from the second floor of the stoa to the classroom building and manufactory behind

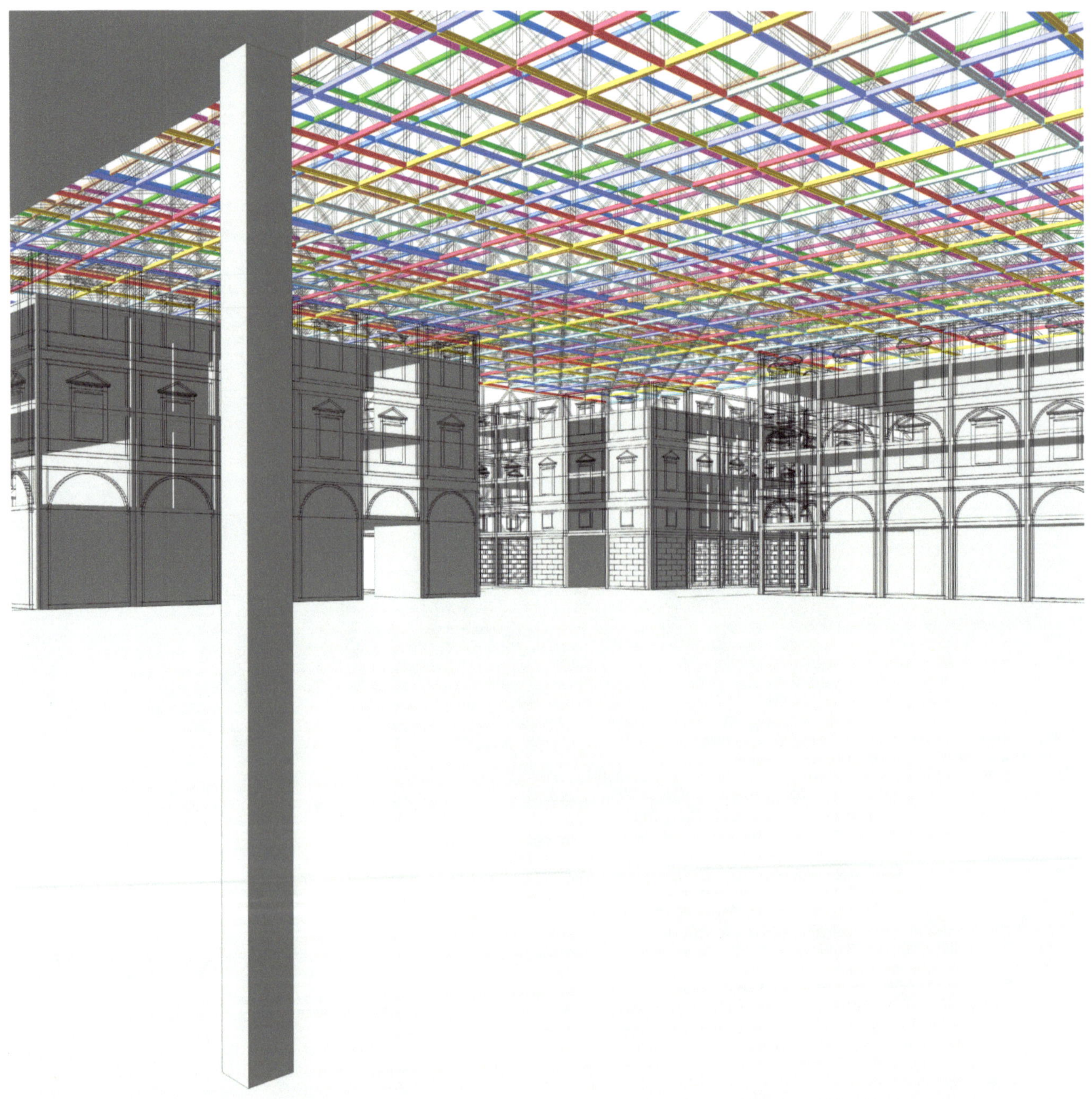

Figure 14. Oblique view looking across the piazza from the stoa undercroft towards the manufactory, library to the right and classroom building to the left

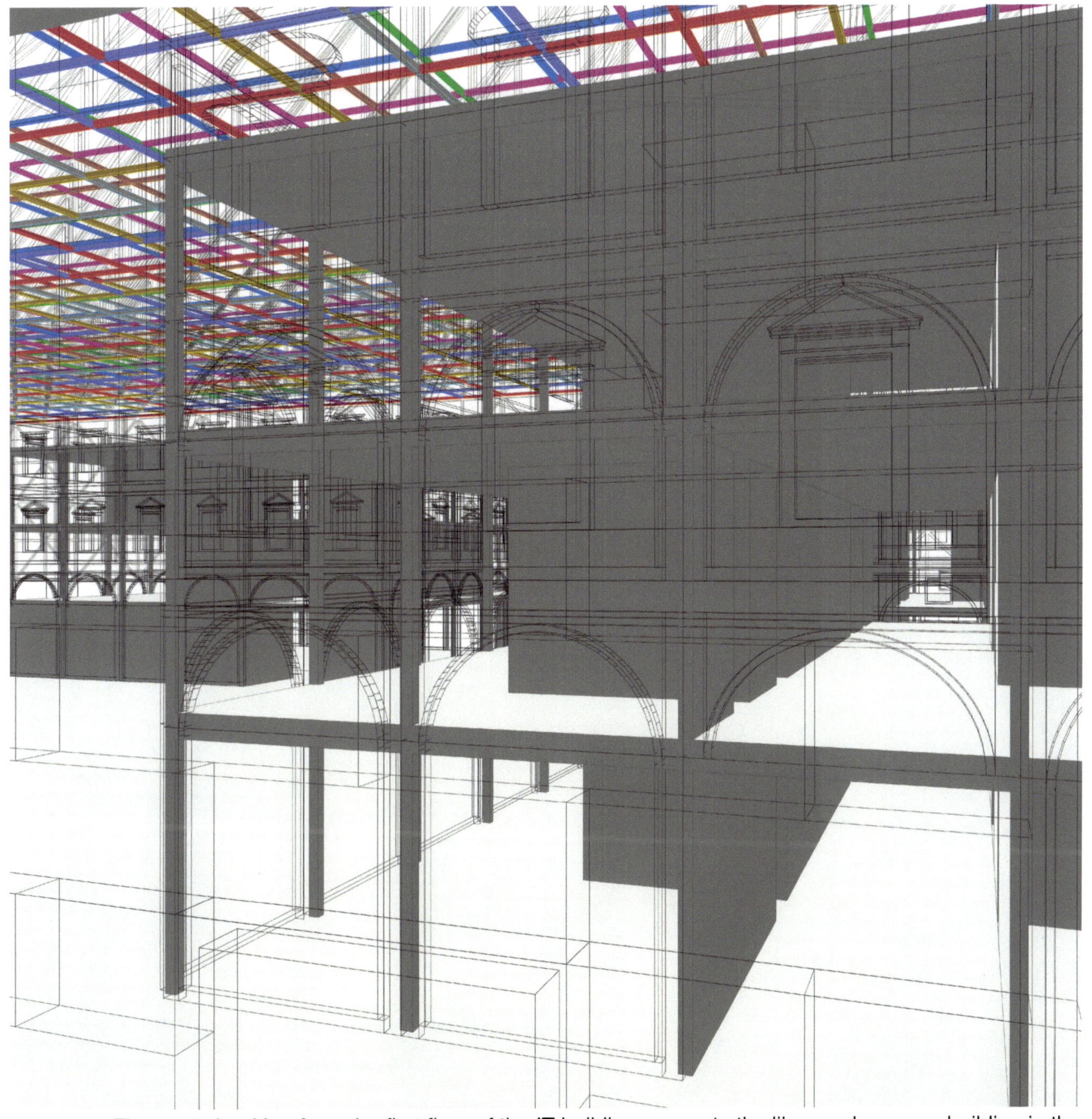

Figure 15. Looking from the first floor of the IT building across to the library, classroom building in the background

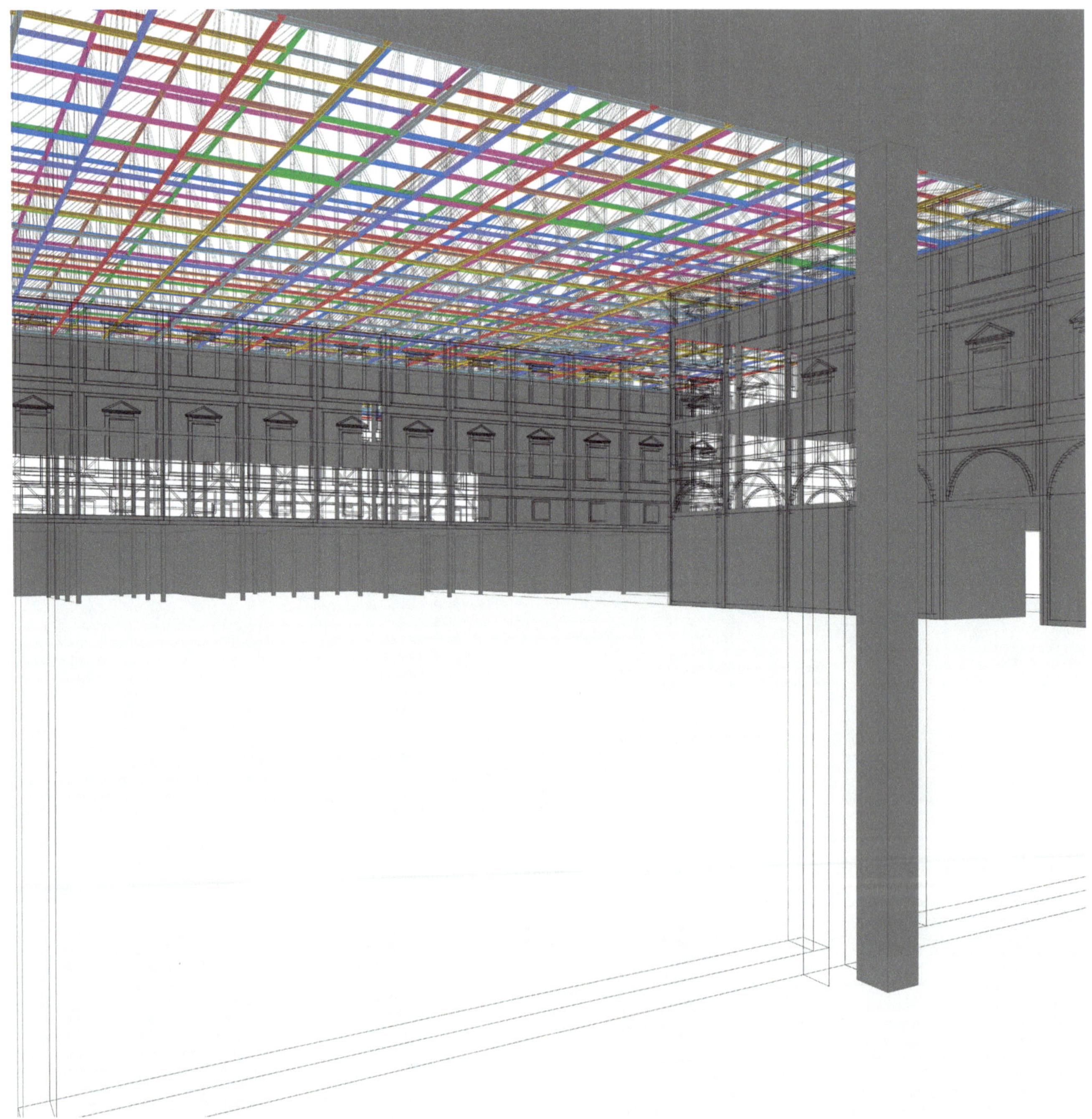

Figure 16. Looking from the library lobby across the piazza to the stoa, classroom building on the right

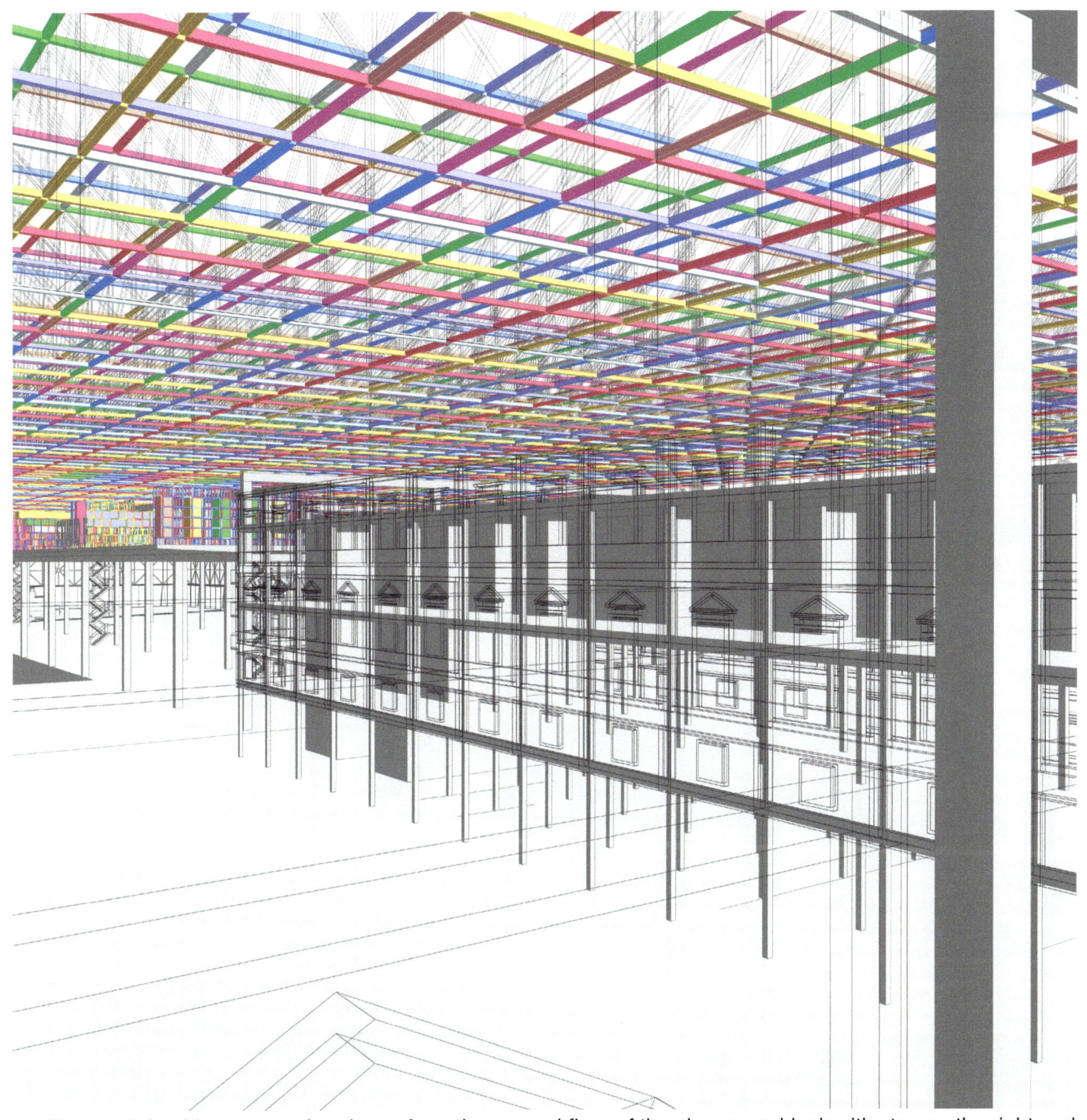

Figure 17. Looking across the piazza from the second floor of the classroom block with stoa on the right and studio and workshop structure in the distance

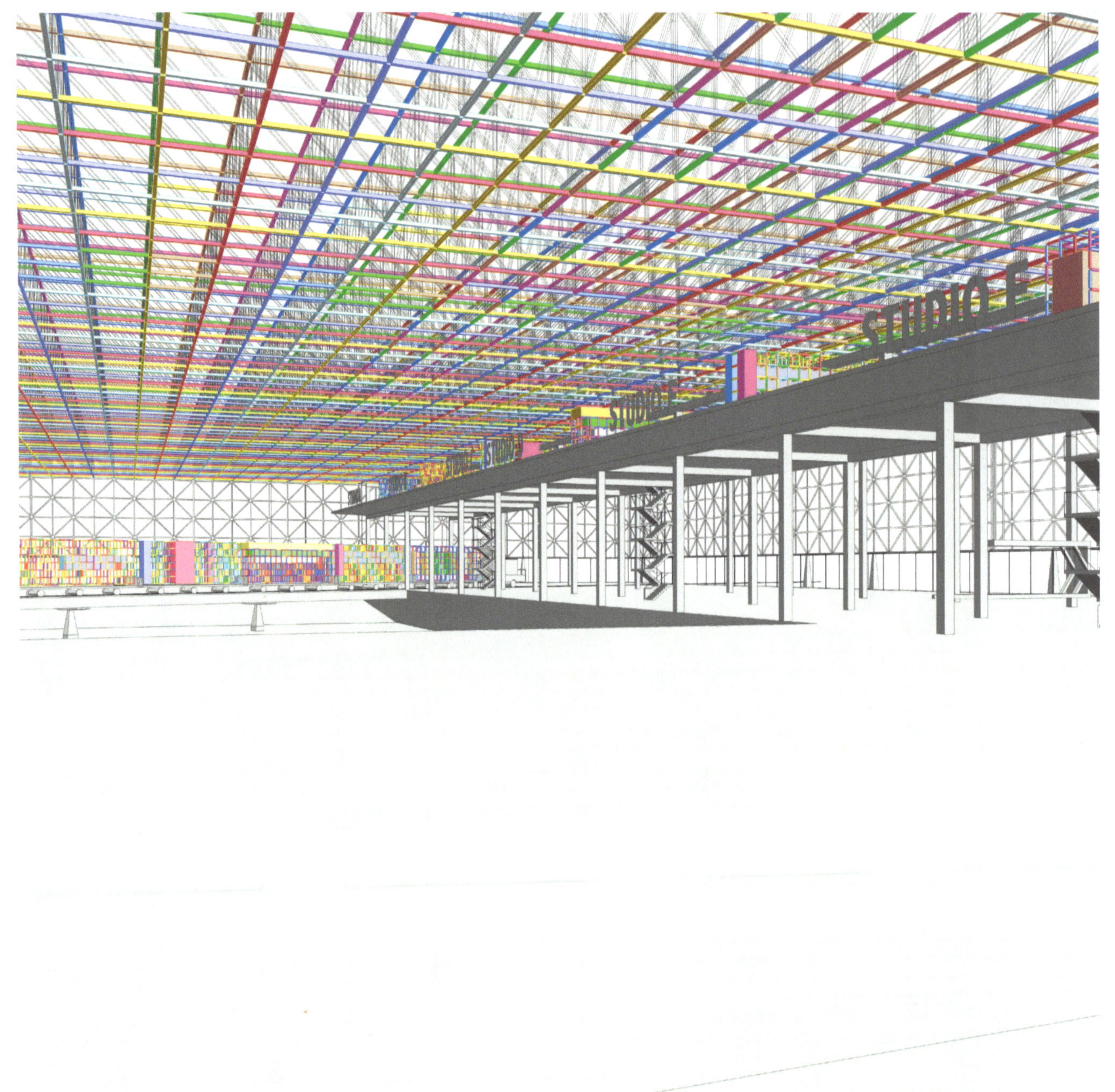

Figure 18. Looking from the piazza toward the studio structure, with departing train pulling out of the station

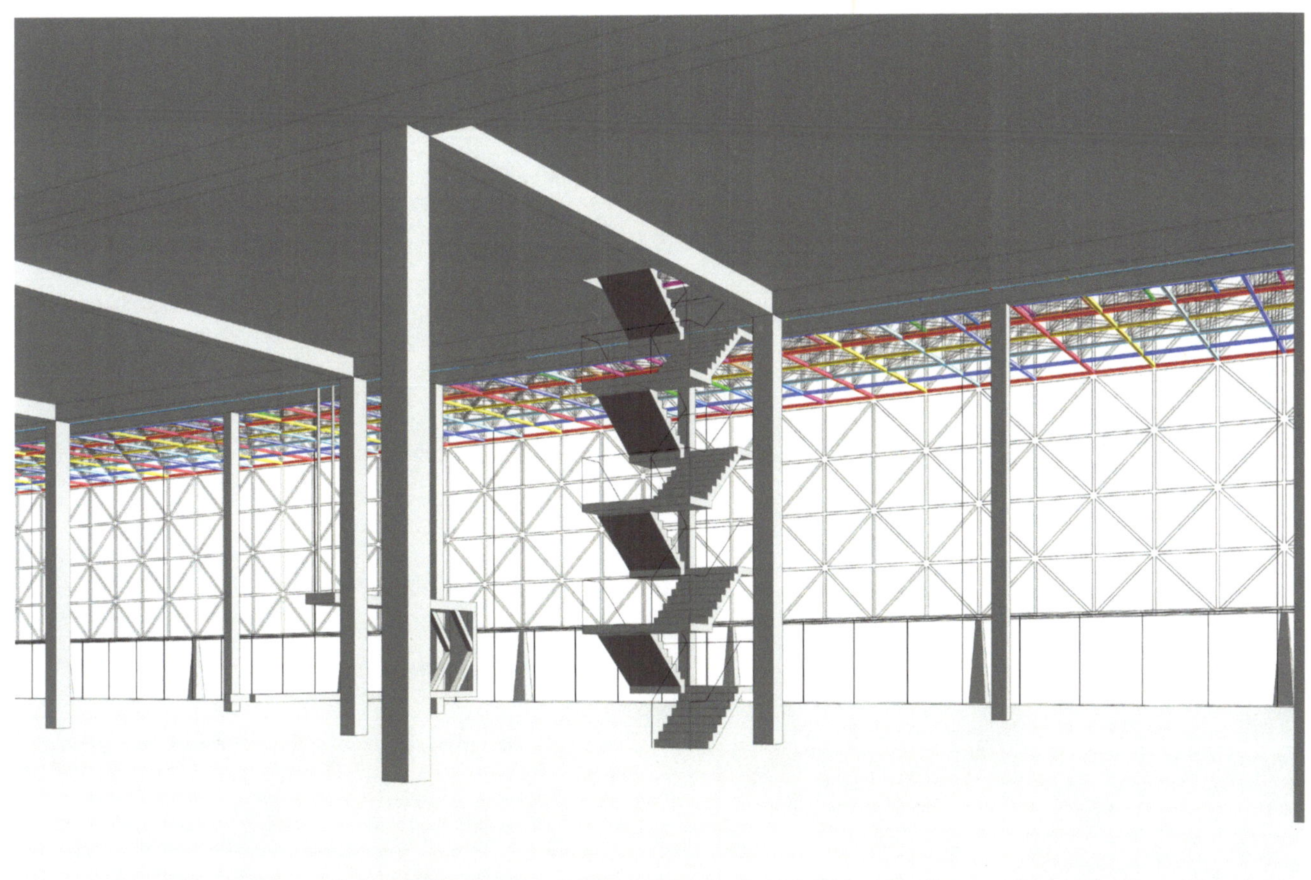

Figure 19. Approaching the studio structure

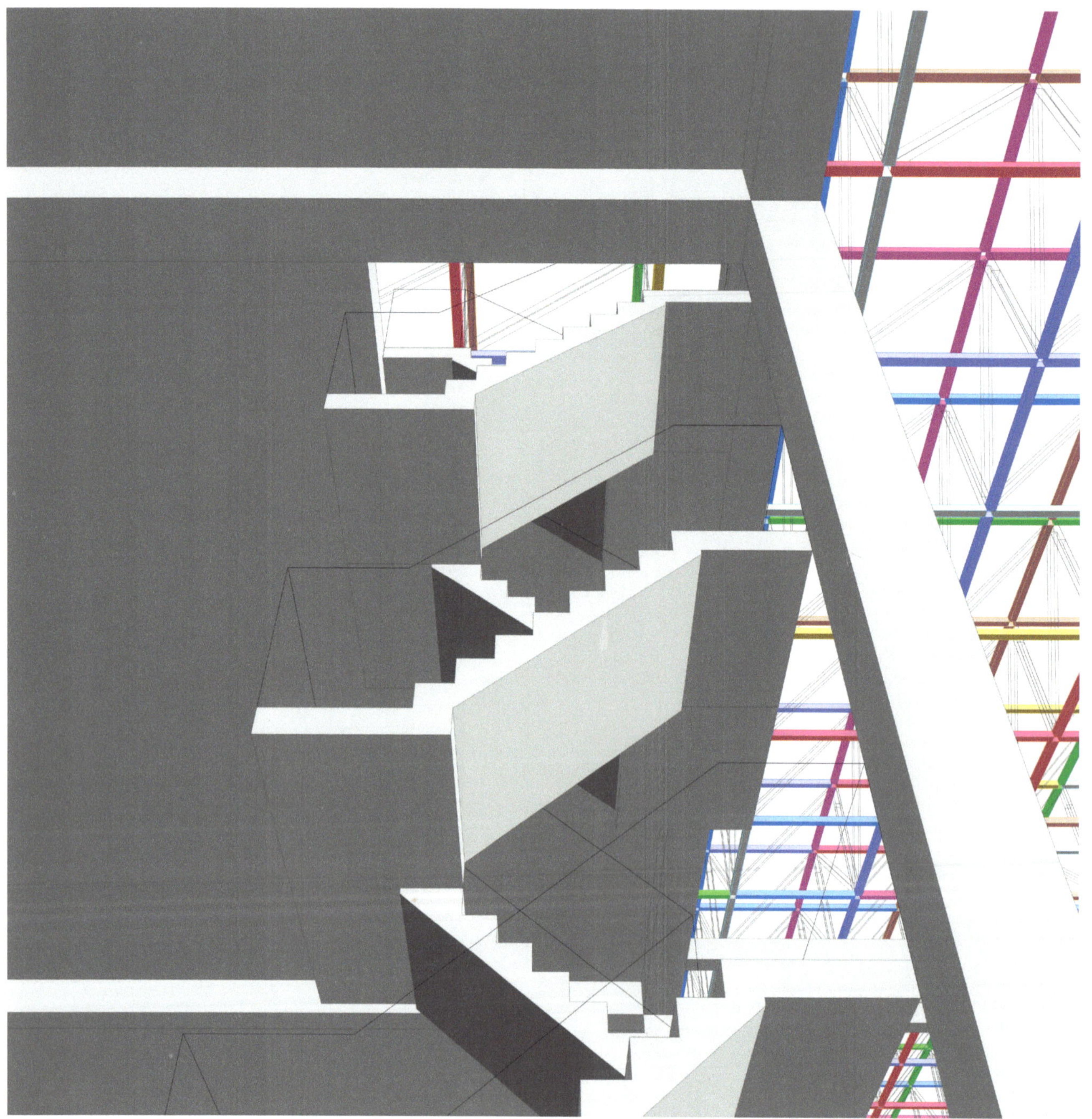

Figure 20. Climbing the stairway up to the studios

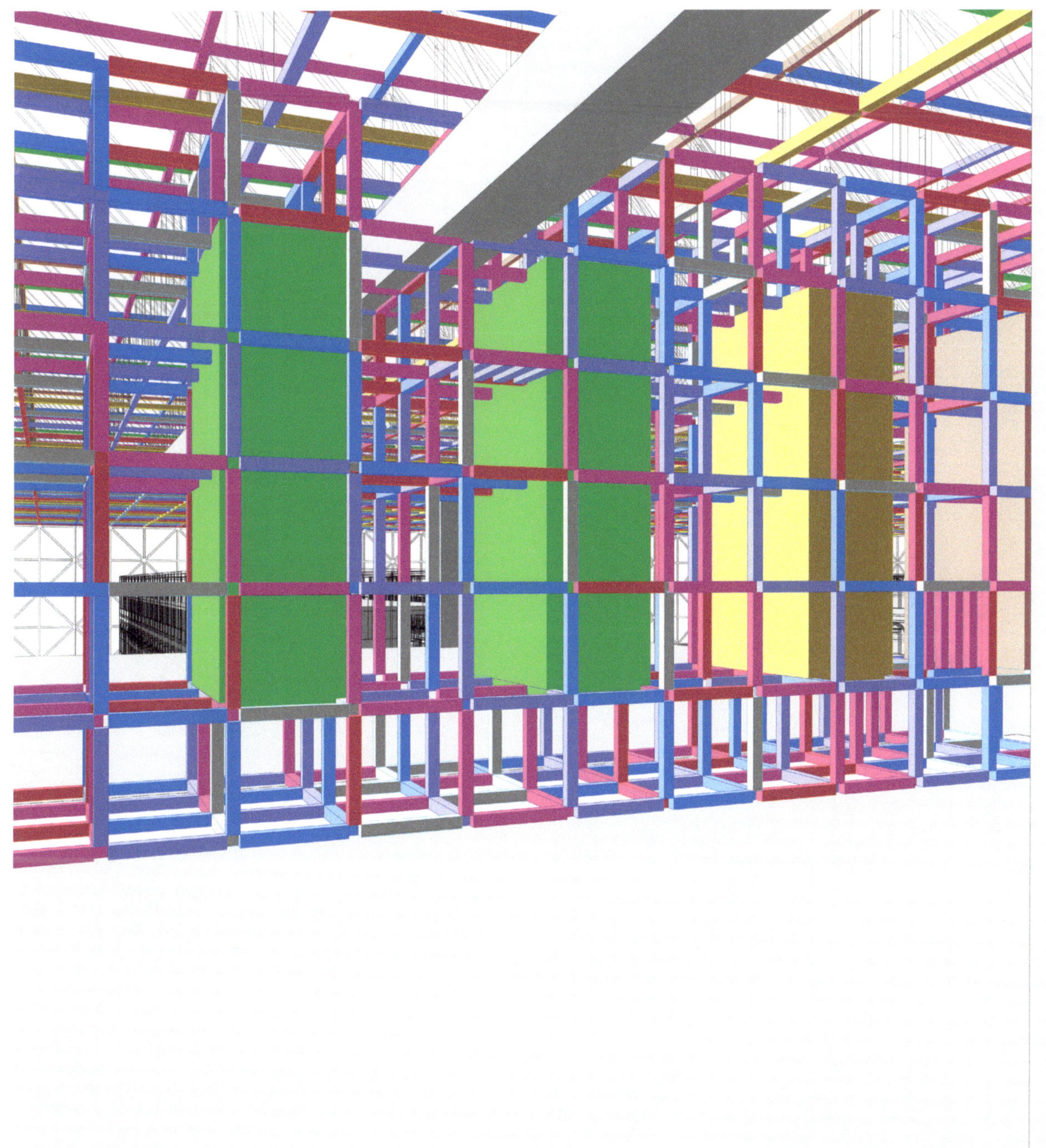

Figure 21. First studio bay

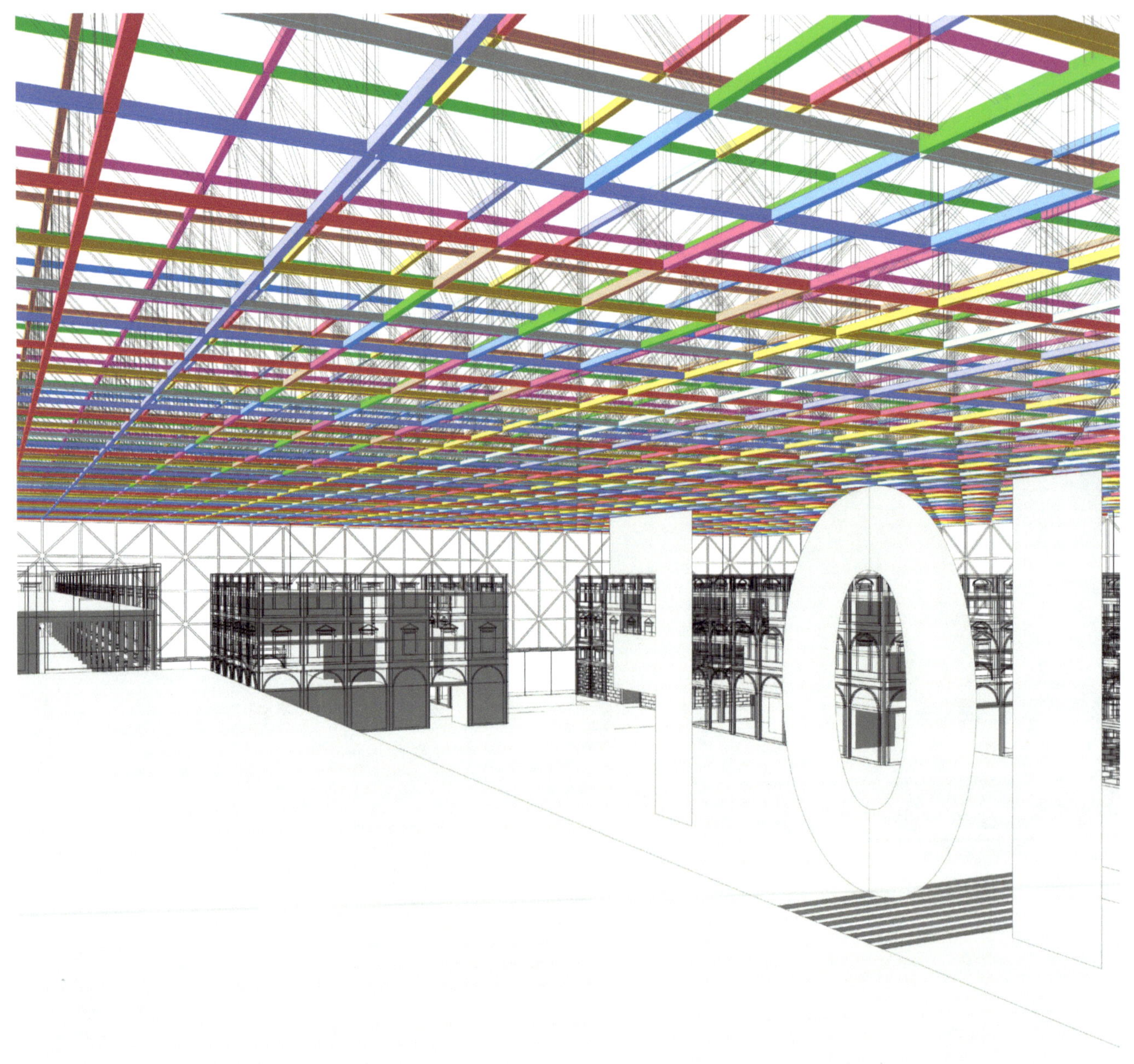

Figure 22. From the studio structure toward the piazza

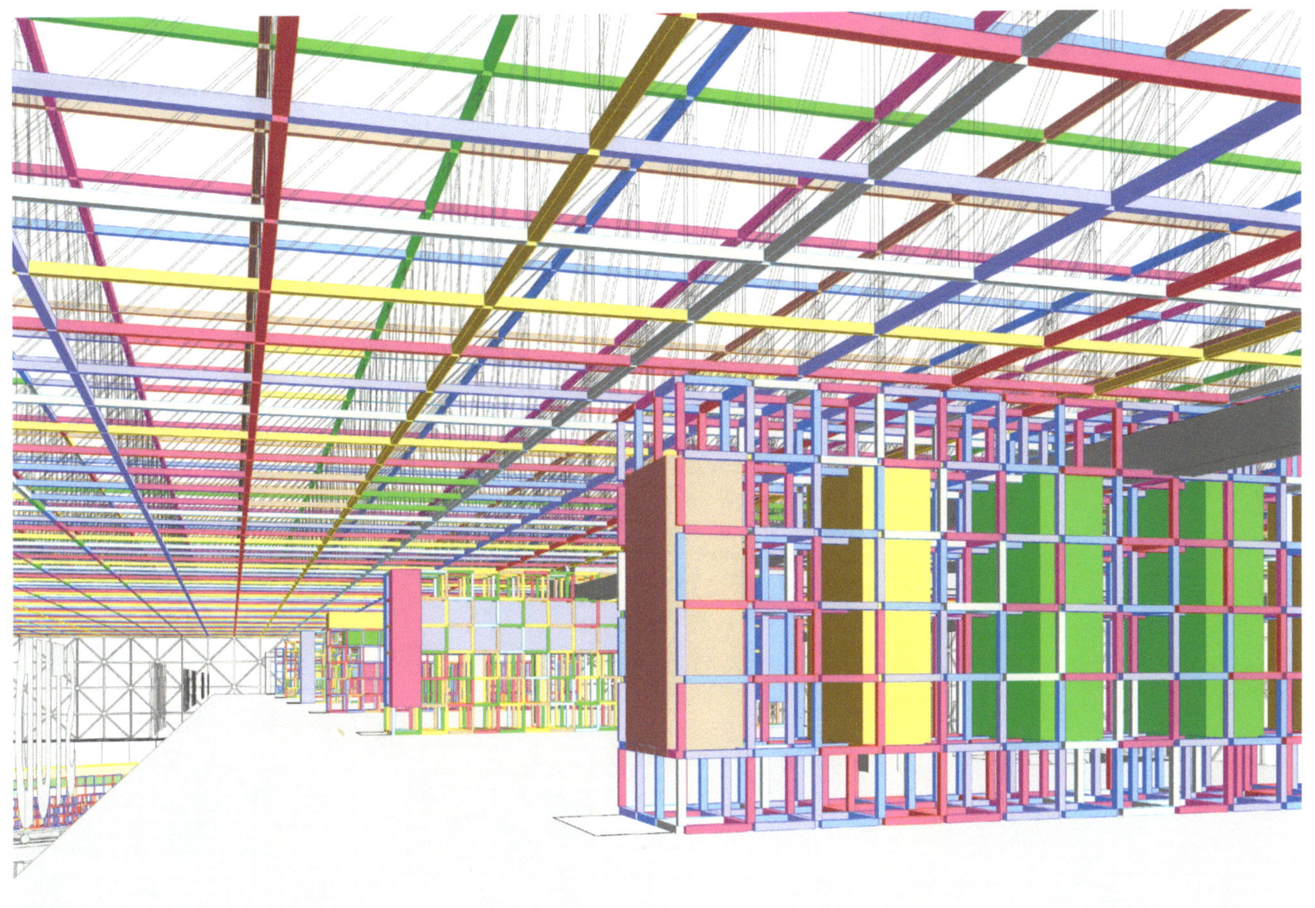

Figure 23. Full length of studio structure, studio bays on the right

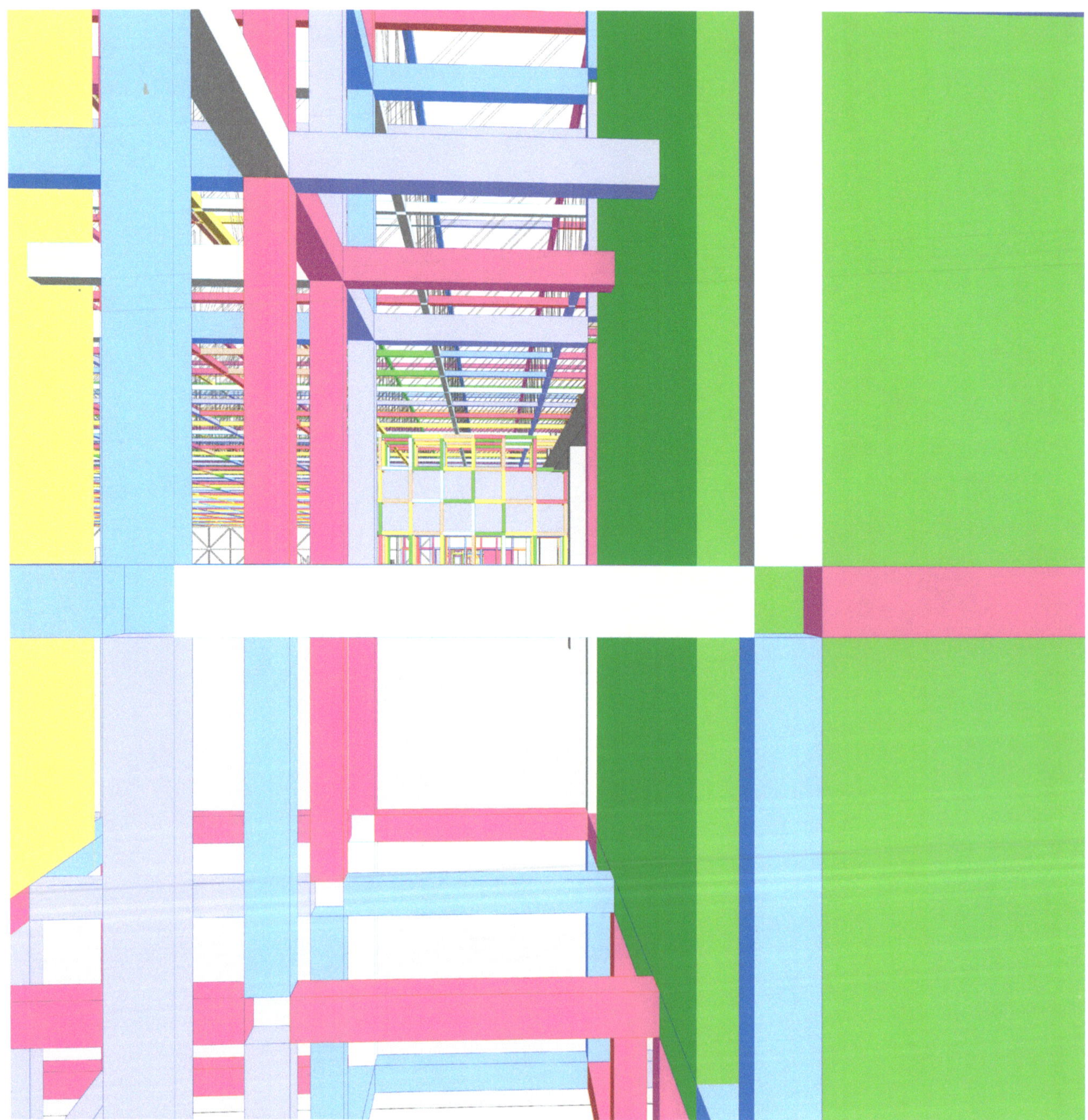

Figure 24. View through studio bays

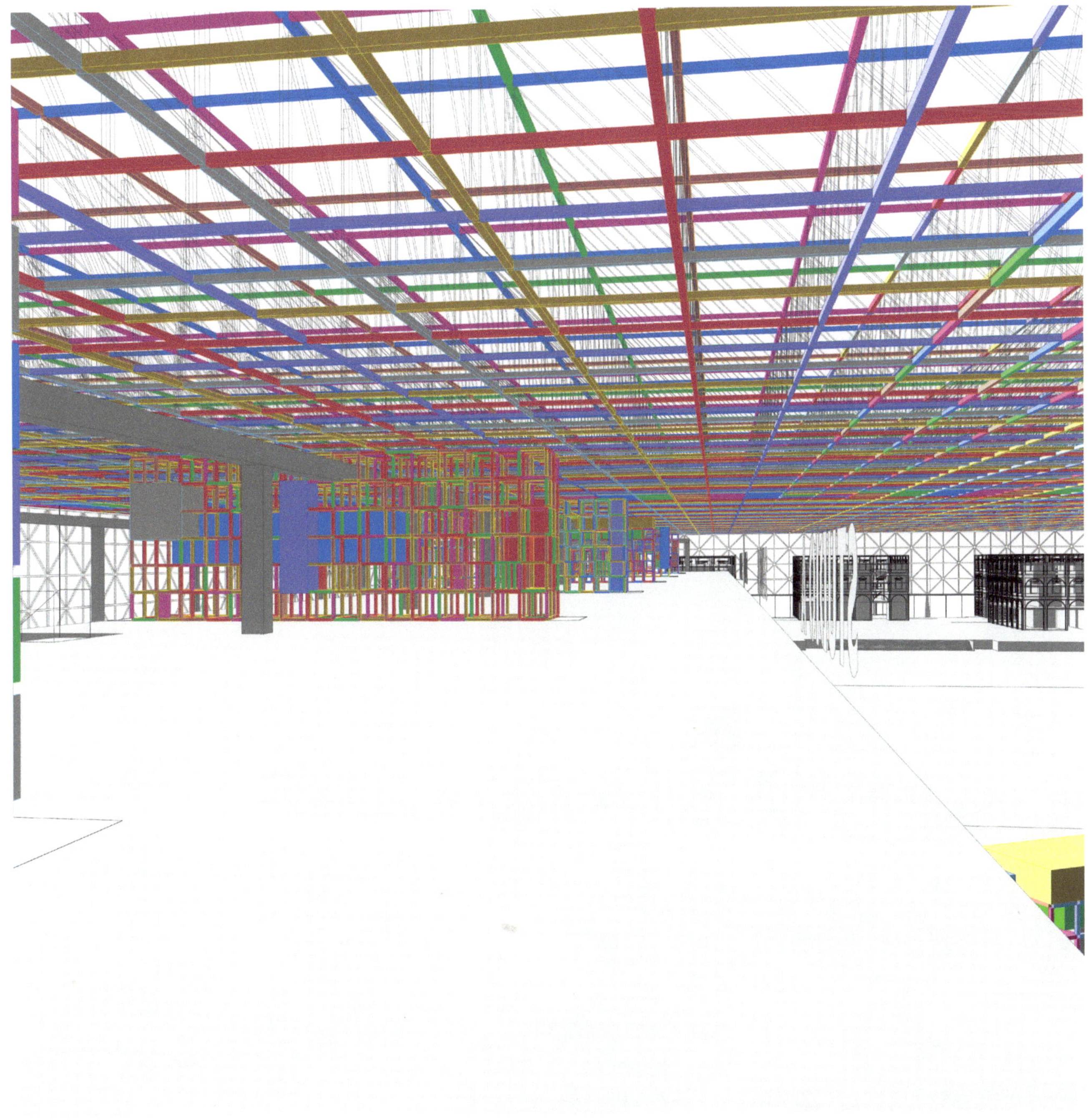

Figure 25. Full length of studio structure, studio bays on the left

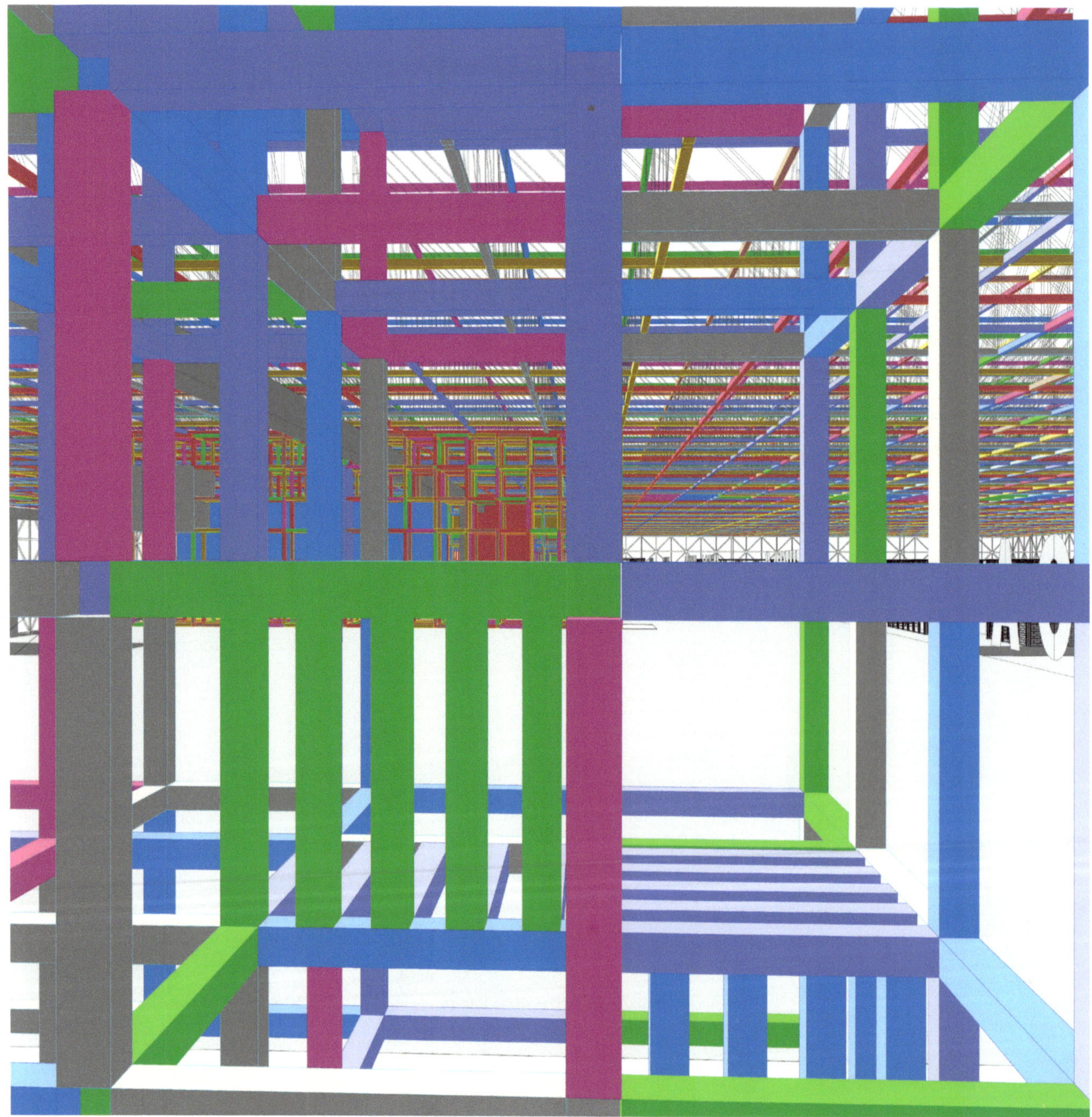

Figure 26. View through studio bays

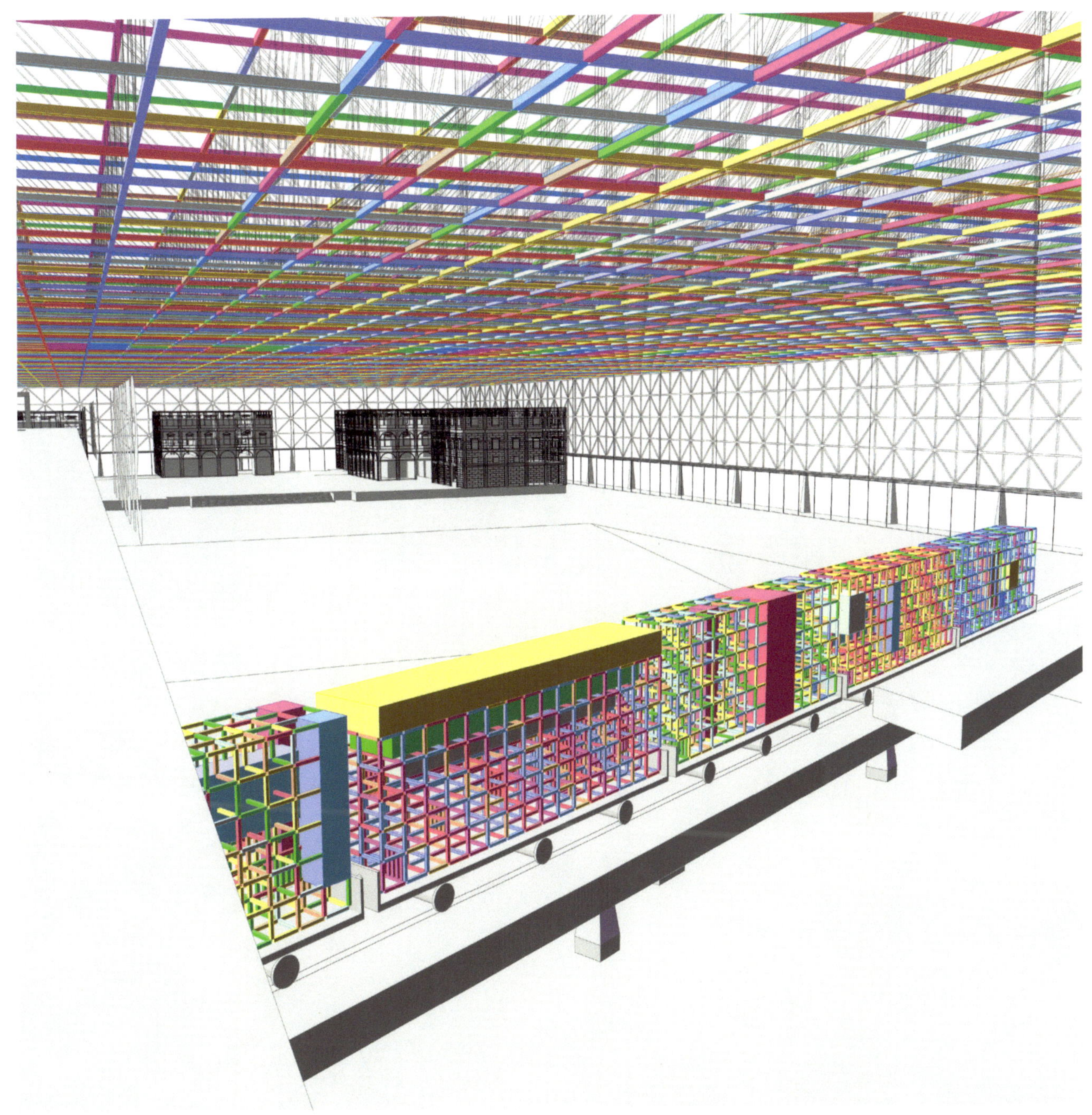

Figure 27. Looking down to a departing train

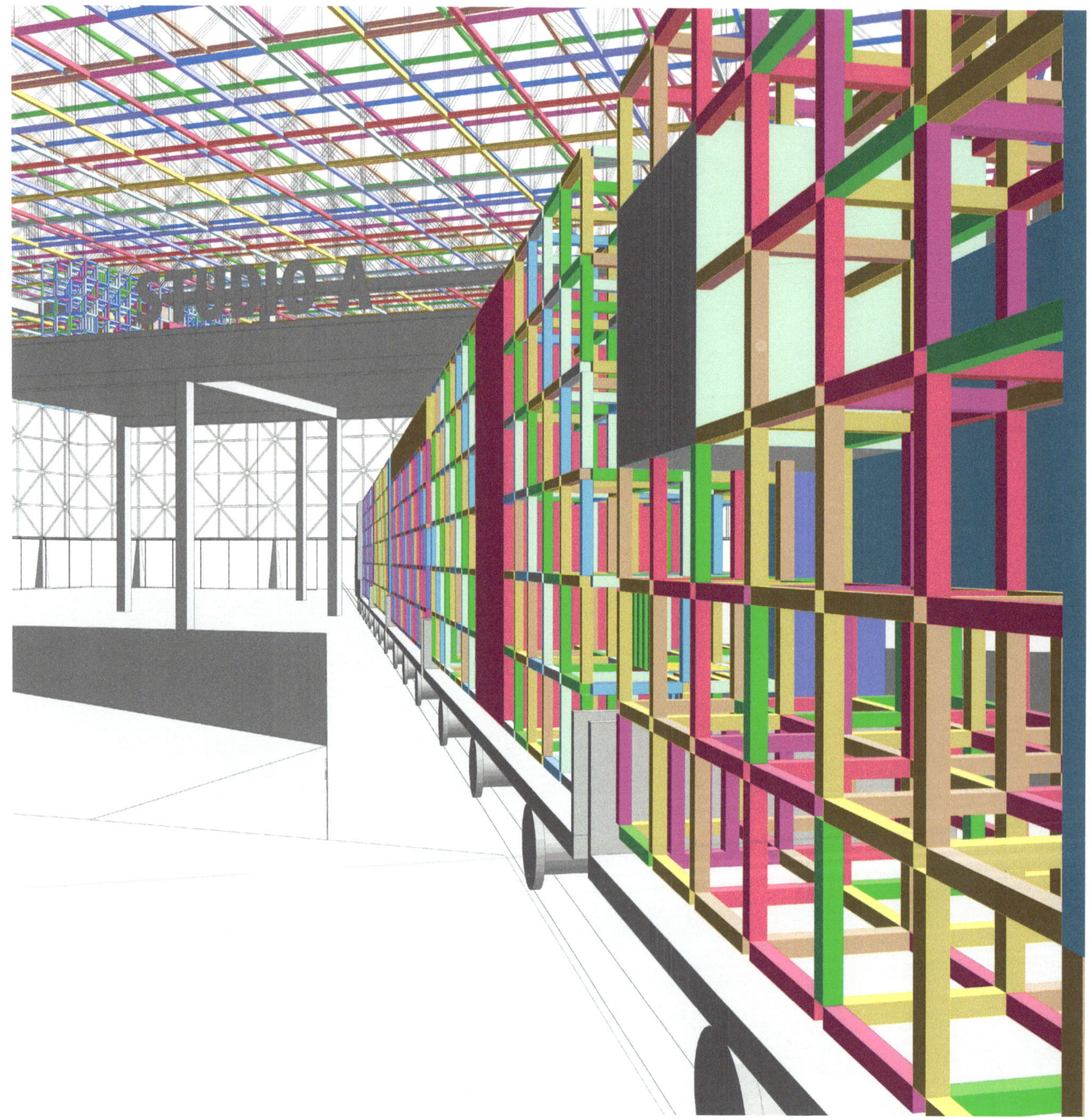

Figure 28. Down on the station platform standing beside the departing train

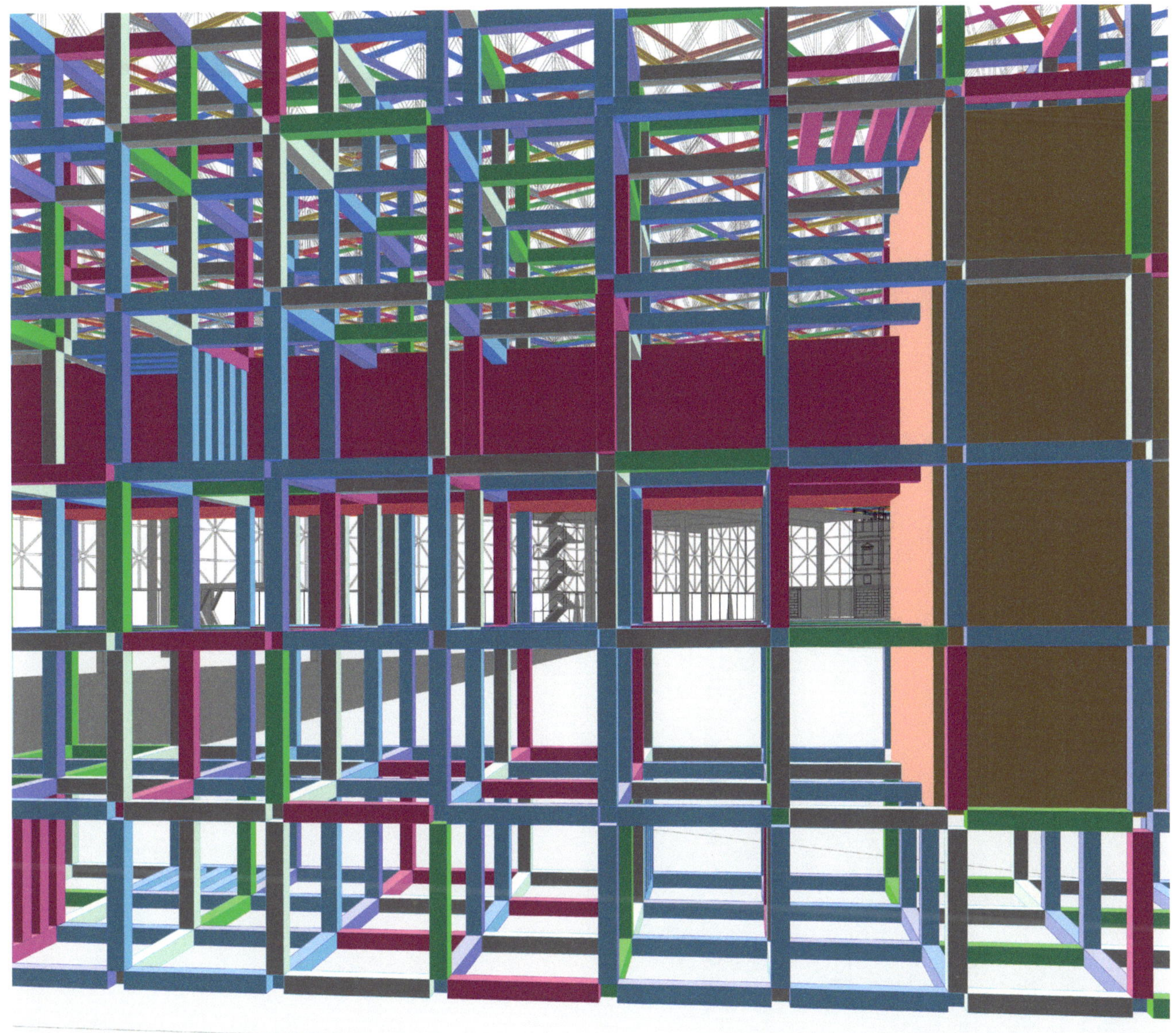

Figure 29. View through one of the carriages on the departing train

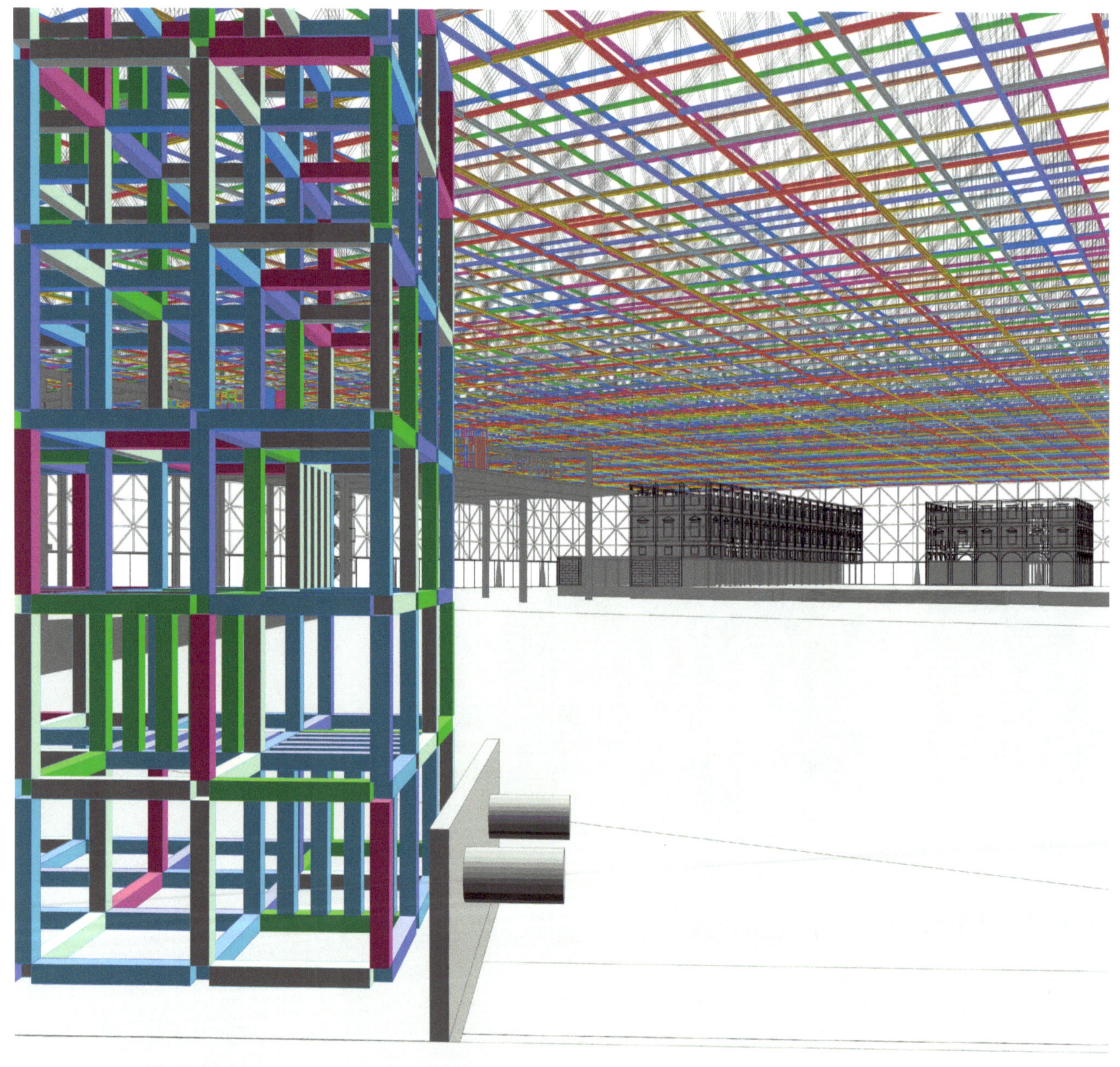

Figure 30. From the platform toward the piazza, train is moving away slowly to the right

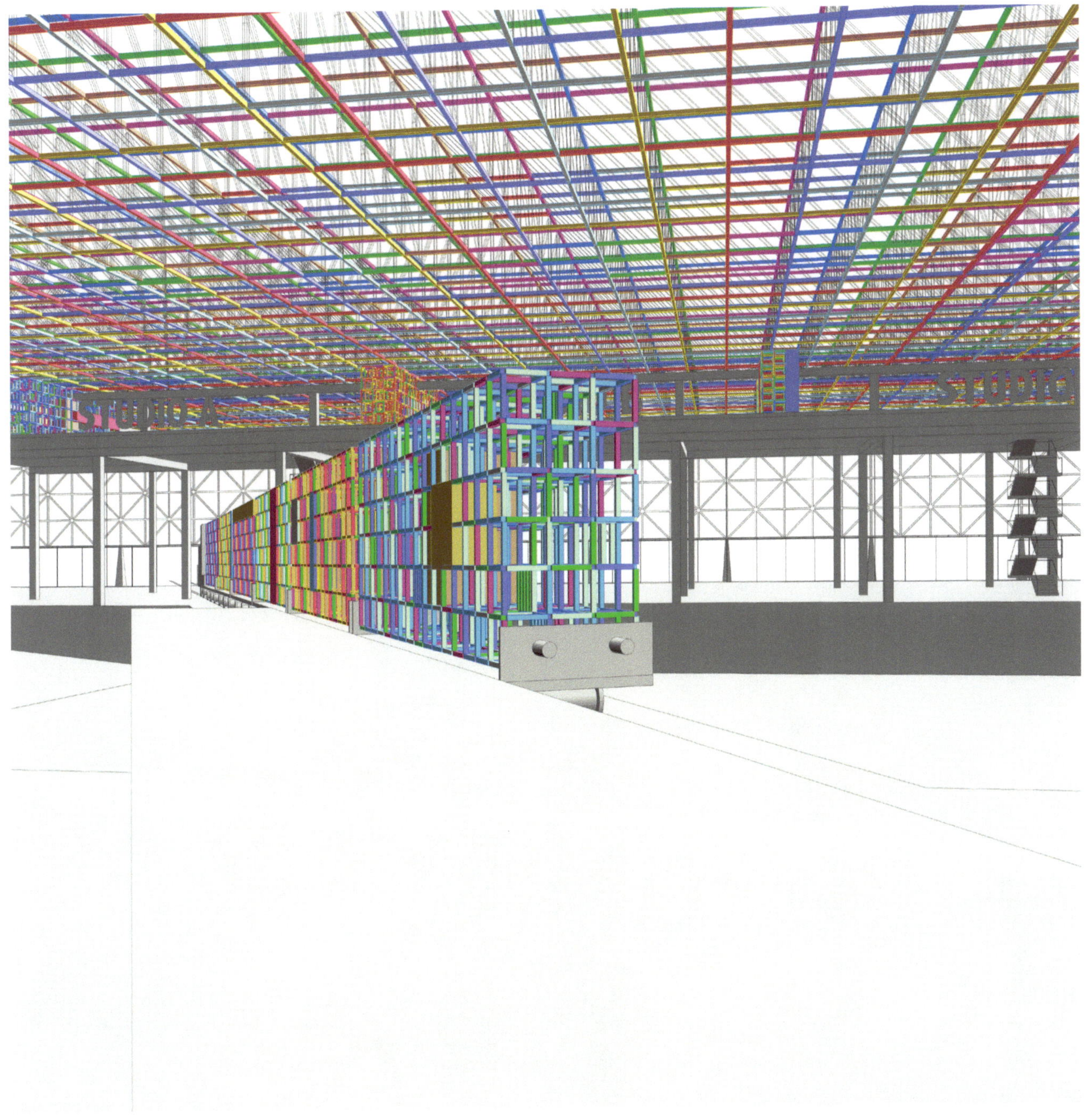

Figure 31. View along platform towards departing train

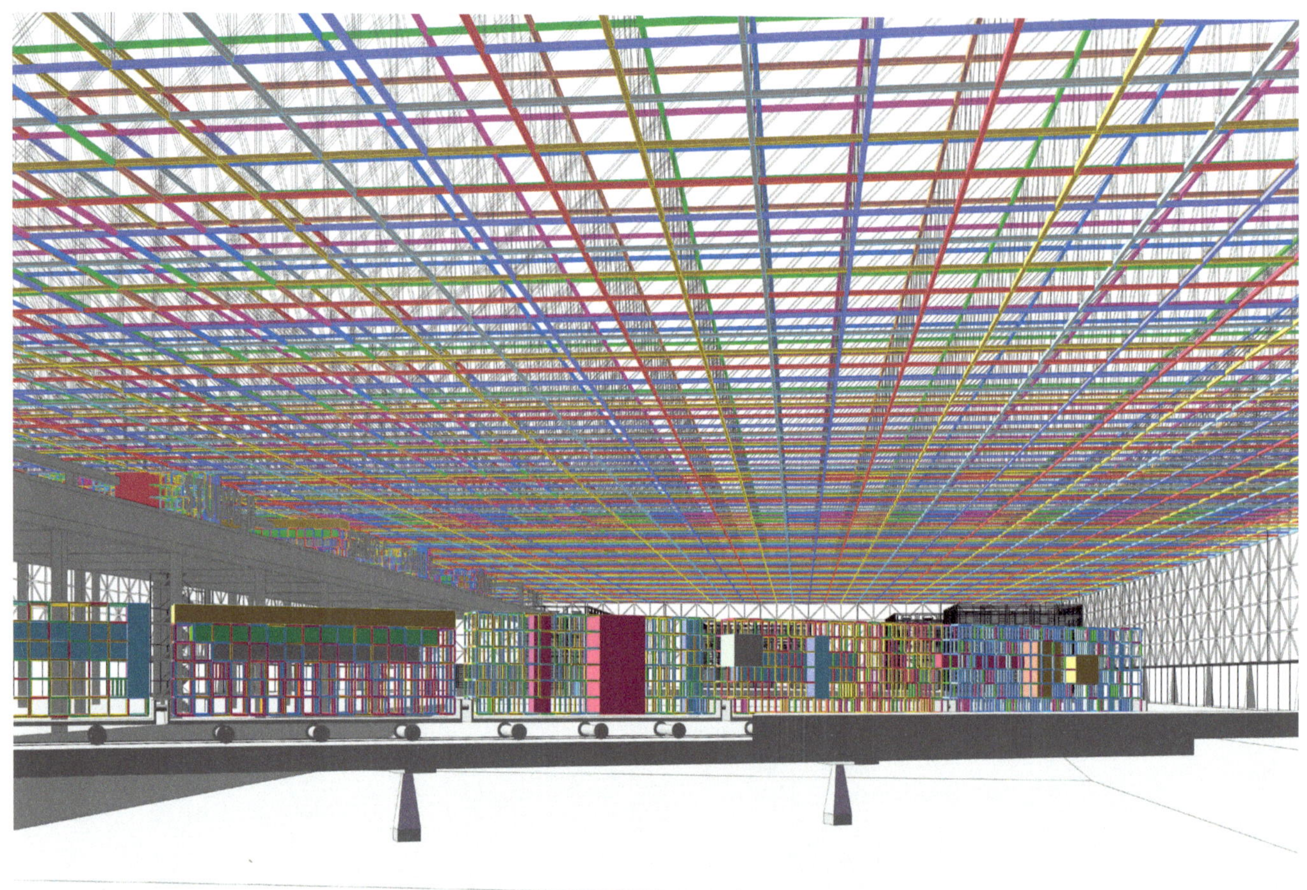

Figure 32. Ramp leading down to station underpass

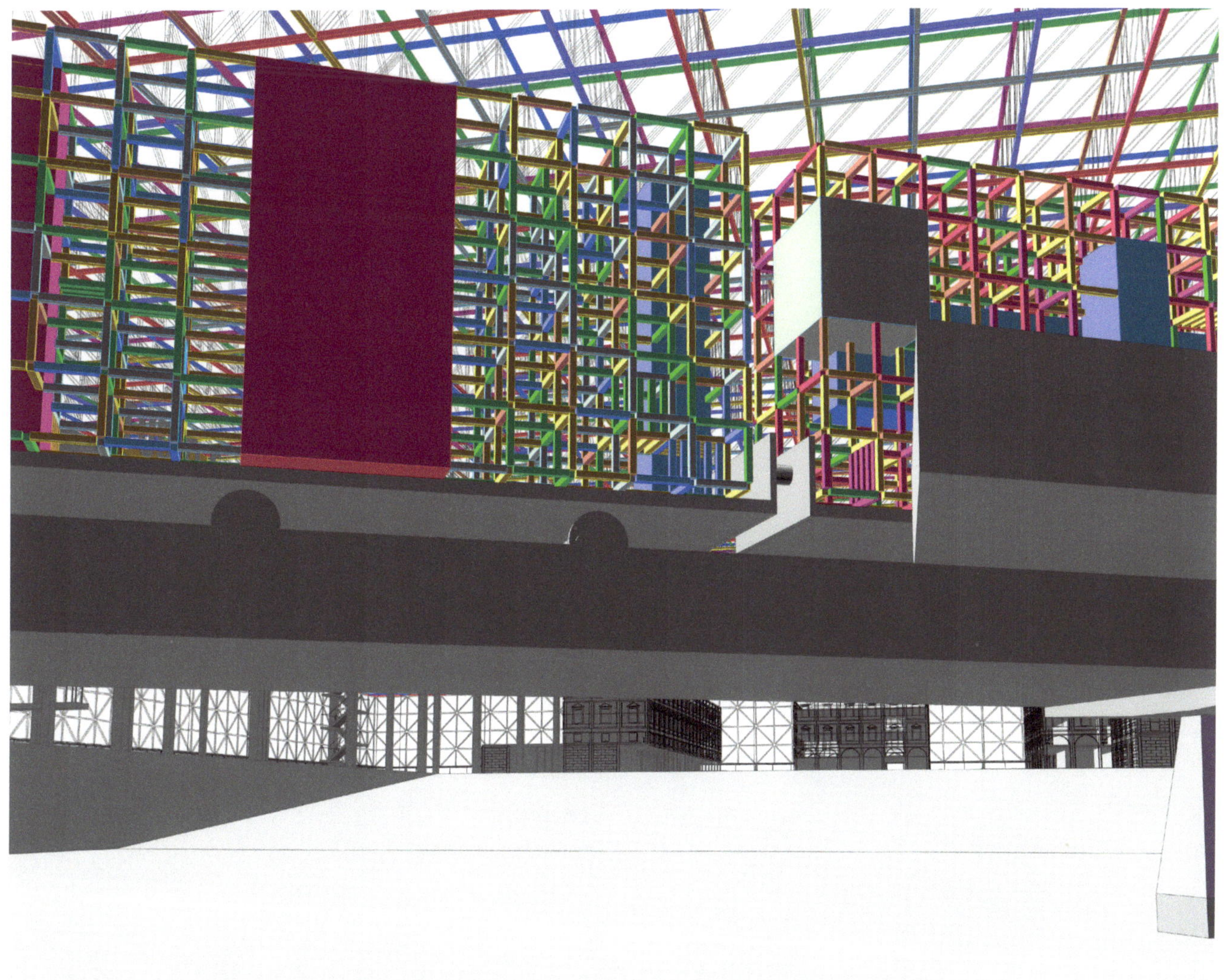

Figure 33. Passing under the station with departing train above

Link to Movie